PRAISE FOR
YOUR PURPOSE IS CALLING

This book is an arrow straight to the heart of a question we all wrestle with: Who is the unique me and how can I make a difference with my one unique life? Personal, compelling, and practical, Dr. Dharius Daniels helps you answer these questions and grasp who you were handcrafted to be.

LEVI LUSKO, founder and lead pastor of
Fresh Life Church

If Dharius Daniels were to write a grocery list, I'd read it! Few people can build such amazing teams, ideas, and accomplishments while remaining connected to their true identity. If you're ready to answer the call of purpose, pick up this book!

JON ACUFF, *New York Times* bestselling author of
Soundtracks: The Surprising Solution to Overthinking

Dharius Daniels has made it his life's work to help others become the best version of themselves, and this book is proof. *Your Purpose Is Calling* is a lifeline to anyone looking for clarity, purpose, and identity. Anyone who reads this book will find confidence that they can become the person God created them to be.

DR. ANITA PHILLIPS, trauma therapist and host of
In the Light podcast

It has often been said that God doesn't make mistakes, but did you know that God also doesn't make extras? God didn't make an extra you or an extra me, because when he decided we were necessary for creation, he endowed us with a unique purpose that only our unique fingerprints can unlock. *Your Purpose Is Calling* is the wake-up call everyone who feels like an "extra" needs because it reminds all of us that the things that make us different were designed by God to make us impactful.

NONA JONES, business executive and author of
Killing Comparison and *Success from the Inside Out*

Dharius Daniels is not only one of the most influential leaders in our nation, but he's also a friend. We've traveled the country together, and one of my greatest privileges is introducing him to our audiences. His credentials speak for themselves, but the words he writes speak even more loudly both on the page and on the stage. As he brings a new level of innovation in faith, he challenges each of us to live fully in ways that will make a difference for everyone.

REGGIE JOINER, founder and CEO of Orange

Discovering your purpose, identifying your distinctiveness, and making your unique contribution to the world is the difference between living a meaningful or an aimless life. In *Your Purpose Is Calling*, Dharius Daniels masterfully unpacks the importance of understanding why God made you the way he has, and how to practically embrace and unleash your God-given potential. You will be equipped and empowered to step up and into your purpose.

CHRISTINE CAINE, founder of A21 and Propel Women

At some point in life, we all reach a place where we question our purpose and destiny. In *Your Purpose Is Calling*, Dr. Dharius Daniels walks us through practical principles to help us identify the gifts inside us that serve as a foundation for purpose. He asks the keen question, "Who do you think you are?" as a springboard into the steps we can take to find that answer, while encouraging us to figure out our "why"—the things that incentivize and motivate us. This is the book my twentysomething-year-old self needed to help me navigate life, and it's the book I need today to keep me focused on my path and calling.

TASHA COBBS LEONARD, Grammy Award–winning
worship pastor and leader

The market is flooded with books on purpose—it's hard to imagine that anything of importance could be said that hasn't already been said. And yet Dr. Daniels has found a fresh way to enlighten us on how to source our individual differences to harness them into a life replete with joy, meaning, and fulfillment. Thoughtfully written, *Your Purpose Is Calling* provides the map, the material, and the milestones and empowers readers to chart their own course to unleash their unique calling and contribution to the world—a destiny reachable through a trifecta of their acquired skills, spiritual gifts, and God-given abilities.

R. A. VERNON, DMin, founder and senior pastor of
The Word Church, Cleveland, Ohio

YOUR
PURPOSE
IS
CALLING

YOUR PURPOSE IS CALLING

YOUR DIFFERENCE
IS YOUR DESTINY

DR. DHARIUS DANIELS

ZONDERVAN BOOKS

ZONDERVAN BOOKS

Your Purpose Is Calling
Copyright © 2022 by Dharius Daniels

Requests for information should be addressed to:
Zondervan, *3900 Sparks Dr. SE, Grand Rapids, Michigan 49546*

Zondervan titles may be purchased in bulk for educational, business, fundraising, or sales promotional use. For information, please email SpecialMarkets@Zondervan.com.

ISBN 978-0-310-36482-5 (audio)

Library of Congress Cataloging-in-Publication Data

Names: Daniels, Dharius, 1979- author.
Title: Your purpose is calling : your difference is your destiny / Dr. Dharius Daniels.
Description: Grand Rapids : Zondervan, 2022. | Summary: "Step into your unique calling in life by embracing your God-given identity. In Your Purpose Is Calling, Dr. Dharius Daniels shows you how God created you to make your specific difference in this world, and the simple key to unlocking your fullest potential lives within you already—your identity in Christ"— Provided by publisher.
Identifiers: LCCN 2022013438 (print) | LCCN 2022013439 (ebook) | ISBN 9780310364795 (hardcover) | ISBN 9780310364818 (ebook)
Subjects: LCSH: Identity (Psychology)—Religious aspects—Christianity. | Individual differences—Religious aspects—Christianity. | Individuality. | Vocation—Christianity. | BISAC: SELF-HELP / Personal Growth / Happiness
Classification: LCC BV4509.5 .D235 2022 (print) | LCC BV4509.5 (ebook) | DDC 248.4—dc23/eng/20220627
LC record available at https://lccn.loc.gov/2022013438
LC ebook record available at https://lccn.loc.gov/2022013439

Published in association with Dupree Miller & Associates, Inc., 4311 Oak Lawn Avenue, Suite 650, Dallas, TX 75219.

Cover design: James W. Hall IV
Cover photo: Jason Good Media Group (jasongoodmediagroup.com)
Interior design: Kait Lamphere

Printed in the United States of America

22 23 24 25 26 27 28 29 30 31 /LSC/ 14 13 12 11 10 9 8 7 6 5 4 3 2 1

To the One who called me, created me,
and crafted me for a specific purpose on this planet.
Thank you, Jesus, for your love, leadership, and lessons.

And to those people all around the world
who in some way have looked to me
as a voice of influence and inspiration.
I'm honored by your trust,
and I pray that I not only make God proud,
but that I also serve you well.

CONTENTS

PART 1: UNDERSTAND

PART 2: EMBRACE

PART 3: UNLEASH

INTRODUCTION

It's been there all your life. Every single day. You've been aware of it for as long as you can recall, and you've resented it for as long as you can remember.

It's part of who you are, but you wish it wasn't. You wish you could clip it like a hangnail and be done with it. Throw it away. At the very least, you wish you could stop thinking about it—just stuff it down deep inside, the way you do bad dreams and unwanted memories.

But you can't. It's like a toothache. The more you try to ignore it, the more you become aware of it. The more you try to pretend, the more you feel overwhelmed by the pain. You roll your tongue against it over and over, constantly confronted by the truth.

You're different.

That's the "it" I'm talking about. That's the reality you can't escape. The part of you that you wish wasn't part of you. It makes you different from everyone else. It makes you stick out. And you've never been able to fix it.

Do you remember when you first became aware of "it"?

1

Probably when you were a child, right? Growing up, the other kids pointed it out all the time. They poked at it. Sometimes they cut against it. Other times they hammered on it. They made sure you understood you were not what they wanted you to be. Not what they expected you to be. You were different. No matter how hard you tried to fall in line—no matter how hard you tried to smooth "it" down or change it or pretend it wasn't there—nothing worked. Nothing allowed you to slip quietly into their queue of conformity.

But it wasn't just a kid thing, was it? Even as an adult, that same cycle is still spinning. Those same expectations are still squeezing.

Don't do that; do this. Don't say that; say this. Don't dress like that; dress like this. Don't look like that; look like this. Don't think like that; think like this. Don't believe that; believe this. Don't buy that; buy this. Don't eat that; eat this.

Other folks seem to fit in naturally. Easily. From your perspective, it feels like everyone else knows how they're supposed to live and just makes it happen without all the fuss. Without all the confusion. Without "it."

You feel stuck with the toothache, and you feel frustrated because you know it will never go away. You just do your best to live with the reality that you're different, and you pretend as much as you can that you're like everyone else.

Because it hurts a little less that way.

But what if there's another way to look at things? What if there's another way to look at "it"? To look at you?

What if the part of you that always stands out is the part of you that lets you stand up? What if the problem you keep trying to solve is actually the solution to something much bigger and much broader than yourself? What if that curse you wish you could cut away is actually a blessing you can bestow on those closest to you? On your community? On the world?

In short, what if that thing that makes you unlike everyone else is valuable precisely because *it makes you unlike everyone else?* What if your difference determines your destiny?

THOUGHTS AND REALITY

"Who do you think you are?"

That phrase usually has a negative connotation in today's culture. It's a challenge. It's confrontational. When someone is getting up in our space or operating outside their area of expertise, we may ask that question as a way to say, "Check yourself." "Step back." "Take a moment to evaluate your actions and attitudes."

Who do you think you are?

Notice the emphasis on the word *think*. We're not asking, "Who are you?"—which is a valid question in and of itself. We're asking, "Who do you *think* you are?" What is your opinion about who you are? Who do you believe yourself to be?

I mention that because it illustrates an important point—namely, that your opinion of who you are isn't necessarily the same thing as the reality of who you are. Those two are connected, of course, but your opinion of who you are can influence the reality of who you are. Sometimes your opinion can even supersede that reality.

To offer an example, we all know people who think of themselves as "less than." Less than lovable. Less than intelligent. Less than competent. Less than attractive. Less than whatever.

Is that reality? No. Each of those individuals has been

handcrafted by the Creator of the universe. Each of those individuals is bursting with potential and blessed with skills, abilities, and talents. Each of those individuals possesses immeasurable value simply because they are members of the human race and image bearers of the Almighty.

That's reality. But when people *believe* themselves to be less than, that belief will supersede their reality.

Here's a principle that lies at the core of this book: Who you think you are plays a critical role in everything you do and everything you experience in your life. Why? Because you will always behave in a way that is consistent with how you view yourself.

Let me repeat that. *You will always behave in a way that is consistent with how you view yourself.*

Do you believe at the core that you are and always will be poor? If so, you're going to live and behave and make decisions as a poor person. The same is true if you believe yourself to be unattractive. Or believe that you don't have a good sense of humor. Or that you're not good at making friends. Or any other convictions that connect with the core of your character.

> **You will always behave in a way that is consistent with how you view yourself.**

Thankfully, the flip side also applies. When you and I believe at the core that we are successful, we will behave in ways that increase our chances of success. When we trust that we are likable and worthy of being loved, we will find ourselves much more comfortable in our closest relationships. When we know in our hearts that God loves us and cares for us, we will live as people who are worthy of that love and care.

I'm not talking about wishful thinking. If you spend a full day telling yourself, *I've got a million dollars in the bank. I've got a million dollars in the bank. I've got a million dollars in the bank—* well, you're going to be disappointed when you check your balance. There is some power in positive thinking, but the idea of sending good vibes to the universe has never been enough. What I am talking about is *identity*. What I'm talking about is your personal assessment of your internal reality, your core convictions about what kind of person you are and what you are capable of achieving.

So let me ask that question again: Who do you think you are?

What do you believe to be true about yourself? What are the key opinions and core principles that serve as the foundation of your sense of self? And how are those beliefs driving and influencing everything you do and everything you experience?

I don't know how you would answer those questions. I don't know who you think you are. But I do know you're correct. Just as the proverb says, "As a man thinks in his heart, so is he" (Proverbs 23:7, my translation).

THE POWER OF YOUR UNIQUE IDENTITY

As a pastor and a coach, I have the regular privilege of interacting with people on a deeper level. A lot of people. Like, tens of thousands over the past twenty years. Walking alongside an individual, a couple, or a family is an honor I take seriously, and I absolutely love the work of digging in to identify and help remove the obstacles holding people back from experiencing genuine transformation and real abundance in their lives.

You know what I've learned after two decades of that

work? Very few people have a strong sense of their own identity. Very few people truly know who they are.

That's a big problem. Why? Because our identity is a foundational element for all the wonderful things each of us is looking for in our lives: meaning, peace, fulfillment, joy, abundance, and so on. Identity is one of the keys in our pockets that helps us unlock all of that and more.

Let's take a moment to focus on an important word that is intimately connected with unique identity. That word is *calling*. If we don't know who we are, how can we understand who we were created to be? How can we fully grasp our gifts and talents and experiences? Identity has a huge impact on personal peace and self-esteem, because those benefits are generated by a proper understanding of who we are.

Here's another critical word: *purpose*. If we don't know who we are, how can we understand what we were created to do? How can we feel certain about our vocation, our reason for being, and the larger goals we are striving to achieve? Identity is intimately connected with our purpose.

If you don't have a strong sense of your identity—the core of who you are—then you are running the risk of living most of your life before you figure out what you're supposed to do with it. You're at risk of continuing to be swallowed up by frustration, confusion, anxiety, and restlessness for another week. Another month. Another year. Another decade.

That's why I've written this book. Because it doesn't have to be that way. It *won't* be that way for you. As we work through these pages together, you're going to discover the power not just of your identity, but of your *unique identity*.

That's key. Because you *are* unique. You are handcrafted and carefully planned by your Creator, which means you are unlike any other person who exists or has ever existed—past, present, and future. You aren't just one in a million; you are one in eight billion and counting.[1]

Yes, you're different. But that's a blessing! Your difference is your superpower. The fact that you are unique means you have something special to offer the world—something only you can deliver. So let's dig in together and discover what that looks like for your life.

TWO PROMISES

Before we move on, I want to make two specific promises about the pages that follow.

This Book Is for *You*

First, this book is for *you*. Specifically and practically.

What I mean is that I haven't written these pages as some kind of academic exercise. As you read, you won't have to plow your way through a pile of generic thoughts or inspect a bunch of information that has no real connection to your everyday life.

Instead, I have specifically designed this book to help *you* understand, embrace, and unleash *your* unique identity.

When I say "understand," I mean we're going to start with your head. I'm going to walk you through the concepts connected with your unique identity in a way that is practical and clear. I'm going to help you explore your *unique design*, your *unique discontent* (what gets on your nerves and drives you to take action), your *unique dreams*, and your *unique destiny*.

When I say "embrace," I mean we're not going to stop with your head; we're going to keep moving to your heart. It's easy to understand a concept that is potentially transformational, but actual transformation will never take place through simple knowledge. I'm going to help you wrap your heart around your unique identity by looking honestly at how you got to where you are and how you plan to change.

When I say "unleash," I mean moving from your head to your heart—and then ultimately to your hands. Which means changing behavior. Changing the way you live. Changing the way you interact with and influence the world. That is the endgame for understanding your unique identity.

Here's the truth. The more you understand your unique identity—the more you know who God created you to be—the more likely you will embrace who you are and the freer you will be to unleash that identity in a way that creates a positive impact in your world.

This Book Is *for* You

My second promise is that this book is *for* you—as in, these pages are "pro you." My goal as we walk through this content is not to criticize or demean you. It's not to shame or stigmatize you. It's not to point out a bunch of stuff you're doing wrong just so I can feel better about myself.

No. I have intentionally structured this book to be both practical and inspirational. Clarifying and encouraging. Illuminating and uplifting.

Forget the stick. These pages are filled with carrots.

I mentioned earlier that I have pastored, counseled, and coached enough people to fill a stadium over the past twenty years, and that's one of the reasons I am for you. I understand the value of support when a person is seeking to make a change.

Another reason I am for you is that I understand what you're experiencing. Personally. I've been where you are and I've lived in those shoes.

Introduction

I know how frustrating it is to feel like the wheels are constantly spinning but I'm not going anywhere, like life isn't clicking the way it should, like I'm not growing the way I should. The good news is that coming to grips with our unique identity will help us gain both traction and transformation. I know how devastating it is to be caught in the comparison trap: she's got it all figured out; his family doesn't have these problems; those people keep getting promoted while I keep sitting here like a chump. When it seems like everyone else is succeeding while you're struggling, I know it's a bitter pill to swallow. Thankfully, grabbing hold of your unique identity will pull you out of that trap and bring you to a place of contentment.

And I surely know what it's like to wrestle with those big questions: *Why am I here? What am I supposed to be doing? Is there some mission or goal I'm supposed to be pursuing?* Trying to do life without answers to these questions is like trying to run a race with weights shackled to your sides. I've been there. But when we *understand, embrace,* and *unleash* our unique identity, we won't just find answers to those questions; we'll find clarity and direction for moving forward.

Finally, I understand what it's like to know deep down that you were born to make a difference and yet to feel impotent and ineffectual because the everyday grind of life keeps sweeping away every opportunity to do something that matters. I hate that sensation of helplessness. Ah, but I love how knowing my unique identity is opening doors for influence and impact in ways I never knew were possible.

The wonderful truth about understanding, embracing, and unleashing your unique identity is that doing so will empower you to make not just *a* difference but *your* difference.

Let's get started!

PART 1

UNDERSTAND

CHAPTER 1

YOUR UNIQUE DESIGN

If I could take everything I want to tell you on the topic of identity and boil it down to just two words, here's what would come out:

Be yourself.

This advice may sound simple, unnecessary, and even a little clichéd, but it's actually quite significant and profound. Here's why. You can't find your purpose until you find yourself. You've been crafted for a specific calling and wired for a specific work. Part of carrying out that calling isn't simply *doing* something; it's *becoming* someone. If you become someone other than who you've been created to become, then you won't be able to do what you've been created to do. Your purpose requires more than your best talents; it requires the best you.

That's the message of this book in a nutshell. We, meaning the world, need *you* to be *yourself.*

I imagine at this point you may be feeling a little frustrated—maybe even puzzled or perplexed. *Be myself? Why do I need to read a book for that? I can't walk down the street these days without seeing a billboard or ride in my car without hearing a commercial or some PSA reminding me to be myself.*

That's true. For my generation, it started with *Sesame Street* and other educational programs we watched as kids. They told us we were special. They told us we were one in a million. They told us we could be anything we wanted to be, do anything we wanted to do, if only we put our minds to it and tried our hardest. They told us to be ourselves.

You and I have continued to hear those kinds of messages for most of our lives. We've been told tolerance is a prime virtue because everybody has differences that need to be respected. We've been told not making anyone feel bad will ensure that everyone feels good. We've been told not to label anything (or anyone) as exceptional because nobody should feel less than exceptional.

Be yourself. You do you.

With all that positivity and all that affirmation, we would expect the world to be in great shape by now. We'd expect people to be self-confident, self-assured, and certain about who they are and where they are going. Right?

Wrong.

According to recent studies, diseases of despair—which include anxiety, depression, substance abuse, suicidal thoughts, and more—are skyrocketing. They've been increasing year after year for more than a decade.

Between 2009 and 2018, suicidal thoughts and behaviors rose 287 percent among people under eighteen. These numbers have tripled in just ten years! Suicidal thoughts and behavior rose 210 percent during the same time period for the age group of eighteen to thirty-four.[1] And remember, all that was before the pandemic.

It's not just suicide. Anxiety disorders affect more than

forty million adults in the United States. That's almost 20 percent of the population. So if you're in a room with nine other people, at least two of them are likely to be dealing with anxiety, depression, social anxiety disorder, posttraumatic stress disorder, or a related illness.[2] I am not ignoring the psychological or genetic factors that contribute to these realities. I am simply arguing that the unspoken and unrealized pressure under which we find ourselves as we navigate life doesn't help.

Then there are alcohol addictions. Drug addictions. Porn addictions. Social media addictions. Video game addictions. So many people in the world today are trying to escape the world.

But why? All of this is bad news, obviously, but why is it happening? Why are we as a culture so burdened and squashed by sadness and despair? Especially when we have put so much effort into telling everyone they are special and worthy of love and respect?

No single answer can satisfy these questions. But I do know *one* probable factor. One reason so many of us are miserable is that we have been prevented from living out of the reality of our authentic selves. We've not been able to be ourselves, and when we can't live the life we were created to live, it causes many of us to feel like our lives aren't worth living.

Another reason we are unable to be ourselves is that we've been subjected to outside forces. The voices of culture and the trap of comparison tend to push against us and prevent us from living authentically. The outside world often says, "Be yourself," but what they really mean is, "Be who *we* expect you to be. Be who *we* want you to be."

Or else.

> The outside world often says, "Be yourself," but what they really mean is, "Be who *we* expect you to be." Or else.

THE PRESSURE TO CONFORM

Society is constantly pressuring us to conform. This push toward conformity starts during childhood, and it's usually quite subtle. We feel it without feeling it. We're shaped by it without any idea that we're being shaped by it. Before long, we get pushed away from the uniquely designed individuals every one of us was created to be.

Think about your own experiences growing up. The adults in your life were almost entirely responsible for your well-being. For most of us, that was a combination of our parents, grandparents, aunts and uncles, and so on. We were dependent on caregivers to meet our basic needs—not just our physical needs but our emotional and relational needs as well.

How did that relationship function? When you did something your caregivers liked, they praised you for it. Maybe they rewarded you. In very real ways, your life was easier when you behaved in ways that pleased them. Conversely, your life became harder when you behaved in ways they did not prefer. If you were too loud or too messy or too physically aggressive, for example, those same caregivers might have scowled at you or deprived you of some privilege.

Pretty quickly we caught on to a basic truth: meeting the expectations of others gained us approval, which ultimately led to acceptance. And oh, we longed for that acceptance! You and I are social beings. We're built for community. And we constantly felt that pull to act in ways that resulted in acceptance rather than punishment.

Please hear me. These realities aren't necessarily bad or sinister. We are talking here about the basic principles of parenting. The adults in your life were charged with transforming you from a helpless child into a functioning member of society, and we can hope they did the best they could do with that responsibility.

Still, the pressure is real. And it's always been there.

These types of pressures continued into higher education and adulthood. If you received training in any area, you were probably asked to do it a certain way. Doctors are trained to practice a certain way; fitness trainers are instructed to train a certain way; entrepreneurs are urged to bring their vision to fruition in a certain way. I am not encouraging you to disregard these best practices. I am saying that just because something is a best practice for them doesn't mean it is best for *you*.

So on the one hand, I encourage you to appreciate those who made a unique investment into your life. On the other hand, I remind you that our differences are not deficiencies.

As you develop and transition from childhood to adulthood, you will be exposed to more and more people. As your community grows, the expectations of that community will grow as well. Not only do loving adults shape our lives, but friends shape us too. Peers. Neighbors. Classmates. For people growing up in more recent generations, those communities now are expanded beyond physical relationships to include online interactions as well. The pool is wider and deeper. And way more dangerous.

Every one of those voices in our pool has an expectation about who we should be. How we should act. What choices we should make. Even when we aren't consciously aware of these expectations, we feel their weight on our shoulders. Pressing down. Pulling this way or that way. Pushing us to move away from our authentic selves and toward what everyone else desires.

Conformity. Uniformity. Homogeneity.

Think of it like stones in a riverbed.

Have you been to a river or a creek recently? If not, I recommend you find a way to make it happen—and soon. Rivers are usually places of true natural beauty, full of life and growth and peace. Standing there, you see greens and blues and grays, all combining and swirling together. You hear the burble and babble of water on rocks. Sometimes it feels like you can actually *smell* things growing.

It's wonderful.

But do me a favor. The next time you stop at a river or a creek, take a moment to gather some of the rocks you find there. If you can, dip your fingers in the water and pull out some stones from under the surface. When you do, you'll notice that every stone is pretty much the same. Yes, some are different colors, and others are different sizes. But every rock you find will follow the same basic pattern: round, smooth, and flat. Slick and cool to the touch. Fits great in the palm of your hand.

Why are all river stones pretty much the same? Because they live in an environment dominated by a current. As the river flows between its banks, the water continually rushes over the stones. Sometimes it scrapes them over sand and silt. Sometimes it cracks them together. Over time, all the edges and identifying features get worn away, and the result is a huge collection of gravel in which each individual piece looks pretty much the same.

When it comes to stones, rivers are places where conformity rules.

The same is true of the relationships and the communities in which you live. Whether or not you think about it this way, you are part of a current. Some of that current is universal within our culture. We all experience it. All of us are constantly exposed to news headlines, articles, tweets, or TV shows that elevate specific values as acceptable and denigrate other values as immoral. We are continually pushed by society at large to behave in ways that its leaders believe are good, noble, or helpful. The flow is relentless. Even ruthless. But much of the current that flows over us and around us is specific to us. It comes from the people with whom we interact, the entertainment choices we make, the ideas we intentionally expose ourselves to, and so on.

Here's an example. I'm a pastor, which means I get the privilege of serving all kinds of people. Back when I first started in ministry, I didn't understand that each of the people I connected with had a specific vision or picture of what they expected a "pastor" to be. My congregation, my staff, my peers—they all expected me to match their priorities and their values.

Which was a challenge! Ultimately, I realized it was a challenge I could not live up to. If I wanted to be effective—not just as a minister but as *myself*—I needed to live as myself. I needed to function out of my own unique identity. I couldn't be the person God made me to be if I was attempting to become the person they expected me to be.

I hear this a lot when I interact with artists, who often feel a similar pull to conform to outside desires. One musician recently told me, "Bro, I want to do something original and creative—something that reflects who I am. But they just want me to make radio hits."

None of this happens directly. There's nobody yelling over our shoulder, "Make this choice!" "Think this way!" "Live that way!"

But it does happen. Every day of our lives, we feel a pressure pushing us to move in a certain direction. To think a certain way. Sometimes we push back against that pressure—sometimes we resist. But have you ever tried to swim against the current? Have you ever tried to walk upstream when the water is deep? It's hard work! It requires a huge expenditure of energy.

That's why most people eventually stop pushing. We learn to go with the flow. To conform. But I want to tell you something. You cannot walk into a full understanding of identity if you are walking with the current. Over time, the current clacks us together and shaves away our rough edges until we become smooth, round stones.

Just like everyone else.

THE REALITY OF YOUR UNIQUE DESIGN

Here's my challenge to you right now, and I hope you will allow this revelation to cause a revolution in your life. You have not been called, crafted, and created to conform; you've been called to reform! Allow me to explain.

Purpose can be defined as the reason for the creation or the existence of a thing. Your purpose is the unique contribution you are supposed to make on earth. The operative term is *unique*. You are not a carbon copy of anyone or anything. When God made you, God did it intentionally, not accidentally. He made you with an assignment in mind, and that assignment is to reform or change some things that only you can. So God designed you with destiny in mind. You can't allow the opinions of people to cause you to miss out on your assignment from God.

In other words, don't conform; reform! Refuse to conform. If you've been going with the flow most of your life, now is the time to stand up. Fight against the current. Yes, it will be hard work. Yes, you risk losing the approval and the acceptance of those around you, but you must still make the effort.

Why? Because you were not created to be like everyone else. You were not created to conform. You were created to be *yourself* in every sense of that word. You are the beneficiary of a *unique design*. That's a term I haven't used yet, so let me back up a little bit and do some explaining.

One of my main goals in this book is helping you see that you have a *unique identity*. As I said in the introduction, you're different. You stand out. You have an identity that goes way beyond the fact that you exist and have a Social Security Number and are part of a specific ethnicity or race and have experiences that set you apart from other people with similar names or similar ethnicities.

This is important. You are uniquely *you* in the sense that nobody else on this planet or any other planet is exactly like you. There has never been, nor will there ever be, another person who is exactly like you. *You have a unique identity.* Not only that, but your unique identity was deliberately calculated and precisely calibrated. You are not the random result of a genetic assembly line. You were planned. You were created. You are a custom order.

You have a unique design.

On a practical level, this means the person you are right now—right this second as you read these words—is the person you were intended to be. To be more specific, you are the person God intended you to be. Yes, there are certainly some areas in which you need to grow, and we'll address that reality later in this chapter. But the fact that your Creator created you means you are not an accident or a mistake.

You are the artistic expression of an all-powerful God.

I hope you'll take a moment to contemplate this reality, because it's a game changer on so many levels.

Take your physical body, for example. For decades now, our culture has tried its very best to squeeze us all into one shape. One size. One look. Even as society has become obsessed with "body positivity," the powers that be are still trying to get you and me to invest in supplements and surgeries and systems and cosmetics and diets and memberships and outfits and all manner of additional products—all so that we can be a little more positive about our positivity.

Does it work? No.

The reality is, you can be yourself while you're trying to change yourself. The next time you stand in front of a mirror, I hope you'll take a second to really study what you see—not through the lens of a fashion photographer, but through the loving eyes of your Creator. Think about the truth that you are intentionally designed. Your hair. Your eyes. Your chin. Your shoulders. Your arms and legs. Your muscles and bones. Your skin and scars. They were all planned. They were all knit together with purpose.

The same is true of your personality. How many people have thrown the word *too* at you recently? Too serious. Too goofy. Too intense. Too analytical. Too ambitious. Too complacent. Too much. Too little.

People who throw "too" at you are evaluating you based on the standard of themselves.

Quick tip. In the majority of circumstances, people who throw "too" at you are evaluating you based on the standard of themselves. They are assessing you based not on the objective merits of your personality but on their expectations of what your personality should be.

Don't give credence to those assessments. Instead, hold on to the truth that your personality is a necessary ingredient in the marvelous and multifaceted recipe I call your *unique design.* The more you try to dial up or dial back the different planes of your personality, the less you are living out of your authentic self.

Be yourself.

Let's not forget talents, skills, and competencies. There are areas of life in which you excel, and you were designed to excel in those areas. Your gifts are gifts because they were *given* to you. Purposefully. Intentionally. As we'll see later in this book, those gifts were given so that you could use them.

Let's also not forget your family. I know that's a difficult word for many people. Families are complex. Families are usually a mix of great joy and great pain, and I'm not here to pronounce any judgments on what your parents did (or didn't do) or to what degree you have been impacted by generational dysfunction, curses, or prejudice. You know the reality of your situation.

What I am here to say is that your family is part of your unique design. More to the point, your family is an *intentional* part of your unique design. I know that, because you would not be who you are if you had not experienced what you experienced—for good and for ill.

I mentioned this earlier but it's worth repeating: there is perhaps no more important fact about you than the fact that you were designed. You were planned. You were intended. That truth should be the foundation of how you view not only yourself, but others as well.

All of us are uniquely designed.

I sometimes picture the concept of unique design as a key. In fact, I encourage you right now to conjure up that image in your mind—a big bronze key with several distinct and dissimilar teeth at one end.

Can you see it? Good. Now imagine filing away those teeth. Imagine taking out a metal file and scraping back and forth and back and forth until the end of the key is cylindrical and smooth. The good news is that you can now insert that key into pretty much every lock. The key has been conformed to such a degree that it fits everywhere. It won't be excluded.

The bad news is that your key no longer opens anything. By filing it into conformity, you have removed its function. You have negated its purpose.

You have made it useless.

You must resist conforming to the expectations of culture and community, because you have a function. You were designed with a purpose. As we'll see in part 3, your unique design means you were created specifically and intentionally to make a difference in this world—not just *a* difference, but *your* difference.

DAVID'S DESIGN

When I think about historical and biblical examples of people who fully embraced their unique design, I can't come up with a better example than David from the Old Testament.

David defied all conventions. He was a shepherd but also a king. He was a giant-slaying warrior but also a poet. He embraced his role as the political and spiritual leader of God's chosen people but also made himself one of those people.

On one occasion, Scripture says that David put on the robe of a priest and joined a crowd of worshipers, "dancing before the Lord with all his might" (2 Samuel 6:14). His wife wasn't pleased with David's behavior because she was more concerned about their public status and the opinion of others. "How the king of Israel has distinguished himself today," she mocked, "going around half-naked in full view of the slave girls of his servants as any vulgar fellow would!" (v. 20).

David's response, however, was grounded in the knowledge of his unique design. "I will celebrate before the LORD," he said. "I will become even more undignified than this, and I will be humiliated in my own eyes. But by these slave girls you spoke of, I will be held in honor" (vv. 21–22).

David was unwilling to be boxed in by the limiting labels of culture. Nobody could pigeonhole him. Why? Because he understood the value of living authentically.

One key aspect of David's unique design was his awareness of God's love and approval. When you read David's psalms—his poetic expressions and songs—what stands out is this: David regularly and unashamedly approached God with unbridled honesty.

"In you, LORD my God, I put my trust," David wrote. "I trust in you; do not let me be put to shame, nor let my enemies triumph over me" (Psalm 25:1–2).

Take a long look at those two sentences. What kind of person gives God orders like that? "Do not let me be put to shame." What kind of person speaks to the all-powerful Creator of the universe with that level of intimacy? With that level of confidence? Sure, it's good to trust God, but aren't we supposed to be hyper-humble when we pray? Aren't we supposed to limit our conversations to spiritual things and topics that benefit other people?

Here's another example from Psalm 139, a famous song: "You have searched me, LORD, and you know me" (v. 1). Have you ever considered the reality that God knows everything about you? Everything. In David's words, "You perceive my thoughts from afar. You discern my going out and my lying down; you are familiar with all my ways" (vv. 2–3).

For most of us, that idea is terrifying. We would prefer to keep some parts of us private. *Can I at least hide my thoughts?*

There are some ideas rattling around in my mind that I don't really want to be judged right now.

Not David. He celebrated the fact that God knew him intimately. Inside and out. According to David, "Such knowledge is too wonderful for me" (v. 6).

Why was David so comfortable standing exposed in front of an all-knowing God? Because David understood the source of his unique design.

Maybe my favorite example of David living out his unique identity comes from his legendary battle with Goliath. Before he could fight the giant, David had to get the green light from King Saul. And even after he received permission, David had to navigate a potentially consequential predicament when Saul invited the young man to use his personal armor—a big sign of honor in that day.

Scripture paints it in this way:

> Then Saul dressed David in his own tunic. He put a coat of armor on him and a bronze helmet on his head. David fastened on his sword over the tunic and tried walking around, because he was not used to them.
>
> "I cannot go in these," he said to Saul, "because I am not used to them." So he took them off. Then he took his staff in his hand, chose five smooth stones from the stream, put them in the pouch of his shepherd's bag and, with his sling in his hand, approached the Philistine. (1 Samuel 17:38–40)

Who tells the king, "Thanks but no thanks"? What kind of shepherd volunteers to fight a giant and then turns up his nose at a warrior's best weapon? "Nah, I'm good with these stones."

Don't miss the dynamic at play here. Armor wasn't the only thing Saul was trying to place on David's shoulders. He wanted David to wear his expectations as well. The king assumed David would fight Goliath like all his other soldiers. (You know, the ones cowering behind the trees each time Goliath started to strut.)

Funny enough, *even Goliath* expected David to fight Goliath like all the other soldiers. The giant seemed offended when David stood in front of him without armor, sword, or shield. "Am I a dog, that you come at me with sticks?" he asked (v. 43).

From every side, people were throwing their own expectations at David—their own assumptions about how he should think and live and fight. Which means that from every side, David felt the pressure to conform.

But he said no. He picked up those five smooth stones, and he fought to make *his* difference in the world by acting out of *his* unique identity.

You and I must do the same if we want to achieve the same results.

THE CONSEQUENCES OF CONFORMITY

What if we don't resist though? What if we choose to embrace conformity instead of rejecting it? What if you and I take the easy path and simply go with the flow as far as it will take us?

What happens then?

Nothing good. I know this from my own life, looking back at those seasons and those spaces in which I allowed expectations to determine my choices. But I also know this from years of experience as a pastor, coach, and mentor. Again and again I have spoken to people who feel this gnawing sense that something is wrong with their lives, though they can't identify it. They are aware that something is missing, but they can't put their finger on it. So they come to me.

And in more cases than I wish to count, the main issue at the root of their problems is a lifestyle of inauthenticity. Of conformity. Of refusing (whether intentionally or unintentionally) to be the women and men they were created to be.

I'll get more specific. Here are three realities you will likely face if you choose to ignore the power and potential of your unique design.

You Won't Be as Happy

I want to say this as plainly as possible. People who live a life of conformity are not happy. Not long term.

Remember, one of the roots of our conformity as a culture is a desire to be accepted. We don't want other people to think of us as different, so we all act the same. We all choose—sometimes even unconsciously—to follow the same rules, strive for the same goals, and make the same choices so we can all accept and approve of one another.

What we don't realize is that most people are unhappy.

Those people you are trying to please by doing what they expect you to do? They're unhappy because they are trying to please other people by doing what those other people expect them to do. They may even be unhappy because they are trying to please you by doing what you expect them to do! It's easy for whole communities to get caught up in this vicious cycle of everyone choosing to be miserable because at least we'll be miserable together.

Here's another thing. It's exhausting to spend a significant portion of each day pretending to be someone you are not.

Literally. Physically. Conformity is a huge drain on so many levels.

Haven't you felt it? You're at work, and you have to spend so much time and mental energy trying to determine what your coworkers expect of you—what your boss expects of you. Then you have to spend more time and energy trying to meet those expectations. You have to come up with new ways to please people. New ways to get noticed without being noticeable.

Then you play the same game at church. And out to lunch with your friends. And on the phone with your in-laws. And on social media with thousands of people you don't really know and don't really care about—but also don't want to offend.

Emotionally exhausting. Physically draining. Counterproductive.

The alternative is simply to be yourself. Your *real* self. No more pretending. No more guessing. No more hoping. Just living authentically as the person you were created to be.

You Won't Be as Healthy

Remember the statistics from the beginning of this chapter about diseases of despair? Conformity leads to unhealthiness on a massive scale.

I'm writing these words in the fall of 2021, and I sincerely hope the COVID-19 pandemic will be a thing of the past by the time you read this book. But even when coronaviruses are no longer part of our news cycle, I know there will still be plenty of pandemics dragging us down as a people.

Like the opioid crisis. Since 1999, more than 760,000 people have died of a drug overdose. Almost a million souls. During the worst weeks of the COVID crisis, Americans were being hospitalized at a rate of about twenty people per one hundred thousand. That number jumped to about seventy per one hundred thousand for people older than sixty-five.[3] Those were scary times, and rightfully so. But check this. In 2016, the national rate of opioid-related hospitalizations was nearly three hundred per one hundred thousand people within the population.[4]

Which is terrifying.

Loneliness is another epidemic in our culture. A recent global survey found that 33 percent of adults worldwide are dealing with loneliness.[5] So if you're in a church meeting with a hundred worshipers, a third of the folks around you struggle with feeling lonely. That's a big deal. According to the Centers for Disease Control and Prevention, "Social isolation significantly increased a person's risk of premature death from all causes, a risk that may rival those of smoking, obesity, and physical inactivity."[6]

I am sure you know where I'm going with this. I'm not saying that conformity is the only cause for addiction, loneliness, depression, anxiety, suicide, or other maladies in today's world. People are complex. You are complex. What I am saying is that it's hard to feel good when you don't feel good about who you are.

You Won't Be as Helpful

When you turn away from your unique design and try to fit in with everyone else, you won't be as happy as you could be, as healthy as you should be, and as helpful as you need to be.

Yes, that word *need* is important. Because the world needs you. Your community needs you. Your family and friends need you. They don't need a copy of someone else. They don't need you to match their expectations or pretend your way toward prominence.

They need you to be you. To be yourself.

Why? Because you are *uniquely designed* to be productive in your family, in your community, and in the world. There are people out there right now dealing with problems that only you can solve. People who require help that only you can give. People who are desperate for something only you can provide.

You were created to make your difference in this world, but you'll never reach your potential if you are unable to accept the truth that *you* are different. You are unique. We're going to explore this theme in much more detail in part 3 and learn about unleashing our unique identity.

THE HARM PRINCIPLE

It's an unfortunate reality that our culture so often labels "differences" among people as "deficiencies." Anything not homogeneous is potentially harmful. The impulse toward homogeneity ought to be resisted. In many ways, the refusal to conform—to resist calling a difference a deficiency—is a revolutionary act.

Still, just because you and I have a unique design doesn't mean we are without flaws. Our world has been corrupted by the reality of sin. Nothing is exactly as our Creator originally intended it to be—including you and me. There are plenty of areas in which we need to grow.

That leads to a big question, though: How can we tell which is which? When there is a part of us that sticks out—when we are noticeably different from others around us—how can we determine whether this difference is positive or negative? How can we be certain that the difference is something we should embrace rather than the outworking of sin in our lives?

The answer is found in what I call the *harm principle*.

We simply need to ask if the difference in question is causing harm—either to others or to ourselves.

Let's say you've got a bit of a temper. You run a little hot at times. That's not a bad thing in and of itself. The world needs people who are driven and passionate—people who are willing to take a stand. Feeling strong emotions, even emotions such as anger, is not a sign that something is wrong with you.

However, if your temper or your anger causes you to lash out in ways that are destructive or abusive, then you are causing harm. The same is true if your emotions begin to damage your own physical health. This points to an opportunity for growth rather than a difference that should be embraced.

Physical health is another example. Your body is a gift from your Creator, and it would be a shame to reject that gift simply because it looks different from other people's bodies. As we saw earlier, your physical features are foundational to your unique design.

Even so, we have the ability to harm ourselves through a wide variety of activities—addiction to exercise, gluttony, stress eating, substance abuse, living an overly sedentary lifestyle, and so on. If your body is harming yourself or others (such as putting your kids' future in jeopardy because you are unhealthy), you should seek to improve it as you are able.

In general, you know when something is harmful. But if there are parts of you that make you feel uncomfortable simply because they are different, you need a new perspective. You need to recognize those parts as elements in your unique design.

When you do, you're going to love yourself more than ever before.

Did you know that the Bible commands you to love yourself? It's true. Jesus identified "love your neighbor as yourself" as the second most important commandment in the entire Bible (Mark 12:31). But loving your neighbor is only half the battle. It all starts with loving yourself.

Here's the reality I want you to recognize at the end of this chapter. You can't love yourself if you're not living as yourself. You can't love yourself when you've lost yourself through conforming to the expectations of others.

That's why understanding your unique identity and unique design is so critical. When you recognize the reality that you have been crafted with purpose, you can love yourself. You can be merciful with yourself. You can show yourself a little grace.

> **You don't need acceptance from others when you can accept who you are.**

Best of all, you don't need acceptance from others when you can accept who you are.

Make that choice today. Accept yourself. Embrace yourself. *Be* yourself. Because you are a special edition. You are one of a kind.

You are *uniquely designed.*

CHAPTER 2

UNIQUE DISCONTENT

Everything should have been great. I should have felt content. That's what people kept telling me.

But in my heart I knew something wasn't right. I *felt* it.

I had been in ministry for several years, and I could point to so many ways that our ministry was thriving. I was leading a large and active church—a healthy church. I was a published author with a track record of success. My family was loving and involved and supportive; we were growing in many ways, including spiritually. Financially, we were stable.

So much was going right. Yet something was wrong.

It's difficult to articulate my feelings from that season. The more I poured myself and my resources into our community, the more I felt as if it wasn't enough. There was a constant sense of pressure to do more. To go further. At the same time, I was aware of a spiritual claustrophobia surrounding my heart and my mind. I felt confined in ways that were uncomfortable. Limited. Squeezed.

Looking back with the benefit of hindsight, I now

understand I was being spurred on by my particular calling. By my unique identity.

From some of the earliest days I can remember, I have wanted to change the world. I have wanted to make my impact on as large of a space and as big of a stage as possible. I felt that desire strongly.

Then I began my journey as a pastor, and I felt that focus sharpening. During my earliest roles in church ministry, I focused on specific assignments within a specific congregation. When I planted my first church, I poured myself into a single community. After all, that's what other pastors did. They ministered primarily or exclusively in the place where they pastored. And if they moved to another church in another state, they changed their focus to that new place and those new people.

That's not how I've been called though. I understand that now. My calling is to create transformational content and lead transformational experiences for the world. For many people in many places. That's why Change Church has multiple campuses—and not just several locations in a single city, but multiple campuses across multiple states.

Do I share this to brag or toot my own horn as a leader? Nope. In a lot of ways, I almost feel behind in my calling and purpose because it took me a while to figure out who I am and what I have been created to do. By God's grace, we are just getting started!

Do I address these issues as a way of throwing shade at pastors or other leaders who stay focused on a single community? Absolutely not. I know and admire pastors who have preached faithfully from the same pulpit for decades. They are spiritual giants who understand their calling and purpose, and I applaud them in every way.

No, I share my earlier feelings of spiritual claustrophobia because that season is one of the first times I can remember experiencing what I call *unique discontent.*

IRRITATION AND AGITATION

What irritates you? I know the answer is probably, "A lot of things," but I'm talking about those situations and circumstances that truly bother you. Like, a lot. What ticks you off? What makes your blood boil?

Pay attention to whatever answers come to mind, because they could be important. In fact, they could be a key to unlocking your unique identity and moving farther down the path toward a life of meaning, purpose, and genuine impact.

Here's a principle: *the problems that agitate you most are more than likely the problems you were created to solve.*

Remember the key premise of this book: You have a unique identity. You are different from everybody else because you were created to be different from everybody else. You were actively and intentionally crafted as one of a kind, which means your purpose in this world is not just about what you do; it's about *who you are.*

> The problems that agitate you most are more than likely the problems you were created to solve.

As we saw in chapter 1, part of your unique identity includes what I call your unique design. You are not an accident. Not even close. Every part of you that matters has been crafted, cultured, and cultivated according to the plan of your Creator. You were built with unique features, and what our society sometimes labels as "rough edges" are actually tools intended to help you make your impact in the world.

As you go through life, then, it's natural for those rough edges to rub up against the world in ways that drive you crazy. Your unique identity gives you a distinctive perspective on the situations you encounter each day. And there will be times when you feel uniquely bothered by those situations—uniquely troubled and upset.

That is your unique discontent at work.

Here's the best I can do in terms of a working definition for this idea: *your unique discontent is a God-given, incessant, unique agitation caused by a specific issue or issues.* Let's take a deeper dive into each of those three concepts.

Your Unique Discontent Is God-Given

First, you need to understand that your unique discontent is rooted directly in your creation. It's connected directly to your Creator.

That's important, because anything connected to God is good.

In today's culture, it's easy to assume we're in the wrong whenever we feel agitated. This is especially true in the church. Many people think they're not supposed to get upset. They're not supposed to be bothered—or at least, they're not supposed to talk about being bothered.

Just stuff it down and keep on rolling, right?

Wrong. It's okay to be irritated by problems that need solving. Actually, it's *important* for people to get irritated by problems that need solving. Otherwise those problems never get solved. What I want you to understand is that the aggravation you feel at the wrongness of the world is often a direct function of the way you were created. It's part of who you are.

Again, the problems that agitate you most are more than likely the problems you were created to solve.

Even during my earliest experiences in ministry, I was genuinely troubled by the troubles of my community. The poverty. The pain. The addictions. The drugs and the dealers. The violence and the victims. It bothered me to see people dealing with so much junk so frequently. That irritation was good. It was right for me to be bothered, and it would have been wrong for me to ignore those feelings and try to just put my head down so I could meet the expectations of everyone else.

My unique discontent was a gift deliberately programmed into my mind and my heart to help me determine my mission in this world.

The same is true for countless people I have engaged and interacted with for the past two decades as a minister, coach, and friend. In fact, I've discovered that one of the best things I can do to serve people is help them embrace their unique discontent.

I know women and men who can't stand the reality that there are children in this world without enough to eat. When they see the commercials on TV featuring rail-thin kids with gaunt faces and haunted eyes, they cannot look away. They *have* to do something—give money, give time, fly overseas and hand-deliver meals if possible. That's their unique discontent at work.

I've also worked with individuals who are uniquely agitated by the idea of people living with no connection to their Creator. Doesn't matter if they know those people or not. Doesn't matter if they like those people or not. Just the notion that the person sitting next to them on an airplane or teaching their children or collecting their garbage might not experience the joy of knowing God is intolerable. Sometimes these individuals possess what the Bible calls the gift of evangelism, but often they are simply driven by their unique discontent. They simply can't sit idly by without sharing their faith.

I've also known people whose unique discontent drives them to care for abused animals. Or visit prisoners. Or buy meals for those experiencing homelessness. Or write books. Or lead worship. Or pick up trash from the side of the road. Or all manner of activities.

Once again, these drives—these examples of unique discontent—are positive. They are a force for good in this world. People who respond to their unique discontent are responding to God-given impulses and reactions, which means they are operating out of their unique identity.

The same will be true for you as you work to identify and live out your unique discontent.

Your Unique Discontent Is Incessant

The second element of your unique discontent is that it doesn't go away. It doesn't fade out over time. Actually, it usually ramps up over time. The problems that agitated you in the past don't just agitate you in the present; now they drive you crazy!

This is important because, as you know, there are plenty of problems in this world. There are plenty of issues that need to be addressed. Therefore it's typical for you and me to feel touched by many of those issues. We watch the news and sigh. We walk down the street and shake our heads. We flip through social media and groan at all the ways our world is going wrong.

But then we move on. We get our morning coffee and feel a little better. We share a laugh with a friend. We catch a glimpse of our spouse as we pull into the driveway, and all the petty annoyances we picked up during a long day at work just melt away. We're home.

That's not unique discontent; that's just being aware of a broken world.

No, you can tell when you're confronted by your unique discontent because you *keep* being confronted by your unique discontent. It's incessant. The grumpiness keeps growing. The agitation continues to accrue. And no matter how hard you try to ignore it, you will eventually get to the place where you can't ignore it. You have to *do something* or risk turning your back on your very self.

That's what I was dealing with during those moments of increasing frustration in my mid-twenties. It didn't stop! No matter how hard I tried to just go with the flow, I couldn't ignore the burden I felt to address those specific issues in my community.

They grabbed hold of me, and they would not let go.

Your Unique Discontent Is Specific to You

The third and final element I want to mention about this concept of unique discontent is that it is—well—*unique*. My unique discontent is specific to me, and your unique discontent will be specific to you.

One thing that really bothered me early on is that so many problems I saw in the community could be solved through education. People couldn't get jobs because they didn't have a diploma. So I started literacy programs in our church building. We brought in ESL teachers. We taught people how to read and how to get their GED. It worked!

It used to bother me that other church leaders didn't value those programs as much as I did. But over time, I realized that they were driven by their own unique discontent. They had issues that grabbed their attention and demanded their time and energy, because *those* were the issues God created *them* to solve.

This is an important point. *You can often tell when you are being confronted by your unique discontent because specific situations bother you way more than they bother those around you.* You find yourself unable to ignore those problems—even as other people ignore them constantly.

When you find yourself in that situation, resist the temptation to try to make those other people feel as bothered as you feel. For one thing, you run the risk of judging others for not conforming to your expectations. I know I was guilty of that during my early years. I started thinking and acting like I was the only person in ministry who truly cared about people. In my mind, I impugned other leaders for "only" focusing on church members and evangelism—which is silly, right? That's what they were called to do.

You also don't need to make other people feel irritated by your unique discontent. It's a waste of energy. It accomplishes nothing—except allowing them to be irritated with *you*.

Instead, when you are confronted by issues and problems that trigger your unique discontent, focus your energy on addressing those issues and solving those problems. After all, that's what you were created to do. Because your unique discontent is specific to you.

"I WOULD NEVER REST"

Several years ago, I first became aware of a school out in Ohio called Wilberforce University. There is a bit of a paradox inherent in that institution. First, Wilberforce University is an HBCU—one of the historically black colleges and universities in the United States. In fact, Wilberforce University is the nation's oldest private HBCU that is owned and operated exclusively by African Americans. The school's history goes all the way back to 1856, which, of course, was before the Civil War. Second, I say Wilberforce University is a bit of a paradox because the institution is named after a man named William Wilberforce, who was British. Oh, and he also died all the way back in 1833.

Oh, and one more thing. William Wilberforce was white.

If you're wondering how a Civil War–era HBCU could be named after a white dude from Great Britain, I was thinking the same thing. So I did a little research. Turns out William Wilberforce was a critical figure in the abolitionist movement of the 1800s, not just in Great Britain, but also around the world (including the United States).

It also turns out William Wilberforce is a fantastic illustration of someone who was driven by his unique discontent.

Some quick backstory. Wilberforce was born into wealth, and he never really intended to do much with his life. He attended St John's College at Cambridge, but he was a poor student. He went into politics as a young man, but in his own words, "The first years in Parliament I did nothing—nothing to any purpose. My own distinction was my darling object."[1]

He was just a guy. One of millions who have lived and worked a bit and had some fun and died.

Things changed when Wilberforce experienced a dark night of the soul—a season of melancholy and gloom that lasted for months. Probably for the first time in his life, he thought seriously about his own unhappiness and his own uselessness. He came out of that season with a deep desire to make something of his life, not for his own sake, but in order to glorify God.

Later, Wilberforce encountered a man named Thomas Clarkson, who was an abolitionist. Clarkson believed the forced enslavement of human beings was a moral blight on the world, and Wilberforce quickly came to the same conclusion. More than that, Wilberforce became determined to confront the evil of slavery. To use language from earlier in this chapter, the injustice and immorality of the slave trade drove him crazy.

In his own words, "So enormous, so dreadful, so irremediable did the trade's wickedness appear that my own mind was completely made up for abolition. Let the consequences be what they would: I from this time determined that I would never rest until I had effected its abolition."[2]

True to his word, he got to work. In 1789, Wilberforce and Clarkson introduced twelve separate resolutions against the slave trade in Parliament. All twelve were defeated. As with America, slavery was a major foundation of the British economy, and the tentacles of those who benefited from that trade ran deep within both the government and the private sector.

Still, Wilberforce pressed forward. He introduced more resolutions in 1791. They were also defeated. He introduced still more in 1792. Those were defeated too. Wilberforce kept going. He authored new legislation proposing to cancel the slave trade in 1793, 1797, 1798, 1799, 1804, and 1805.

All were voted down.

Can you imagine how tempting it must have been for someone in Wilberforce's position to give up at that point? For one thing, he wasn't personally impacted by slavery or the slave trade. He wasn't losing any money, and it's unlikely he had personal knowledge of or interactions with the people who were impacted most.

For another thing, it's not like he hadn't tried! He had

devoted *decades* of his life to this cause. He'd trashed his reputation among many in "sophisticated" society by continuing to focus on this issue. He'd jeopardized his own career. I'm sure there were people in his ear advising him to focus on something else. "You tried, Bill. Let it go."

But that's just it. Wilberforce could not let it go. He was driven, not just by personal convictions about right and wrong, but by his unique discontent. In some ways, he couldn't help it. He *had* to address the problem he was created to solve.

Finally, in 1807, William Wilberforce and his allies broke through. Parliament passed a law making the slave trade illegal within the British Empire. It's hard to overstate the magnitude of that moment, but it was literally life-changing for millions of people. In many ways, that law was the death knell for legalized slavery around the world.

Even so, Wilberforce kept working. His next goal was making sure the new laws were enforced—no small task. Then he spent another decade seeking the abolishment not just of the slave trade but of slavery itself. He worked toward winning legal freedom for those who had previously been sold as slaves.

Wilberforce died in 1833—just three days after learning that Parliament had passed the bill to finally and officially abolish slavery in the British Empire. I love the idea that he went to his eternal home knowing that his life's work was successful. The problem he was created to solve was actually beginning to be solved, not just in his home country, but around the world.

I share this story because it illustrates an important point about our unique discontent—namely, that we're not talking about something minor, something that bothers us on the level of a neighbor's dog doing its business in our yard.

No, your unique discontent will be a major source of

passion and provocation in your life. And when you embrace that passion, it can drive you to accomplish incredible things.

"I SAT DOWN AND WEPT"

Right about now you may be thinking, *So what?*

You understand what I'm pointing out with this concept of unique discontent. Maybe you even agree with this idea in principle. You see what I'm saying. But you're wondering how it applies to you. *What difference can embracing my unique discontent make in my life? Now that I know what it is, what am I supposed to do about it?*

Good questions. To finish out this chapter, I want to answer these questions by quickly exploring the life of a man named Nehemiah from the Old Testament.

In case you've never heard that name, Nehemiah was an Israelite man living far away from his homeland. Around 586 BC, the Babylonian army destroyed the city of Jerusalem, burned Solomon's temple to the ground, and took many Israelites captive. The Babylonian king, Nebuchadnezzar, took those captives back to Babylon, where many of them served as slaves. Those who were nobles in Jerusalem were educated and allowed to take positions in the Babylonian government.[3]

About 150 years later, Nehemiah served as the cupbearer to another foreign king, Artaxerxes of Persia. (The Persians had conquered Babylon decades earlier.) Nehemiah was the descendant of Israelite exiles, which means he had never set foot in Israel or Jerusalem. He was raised as a stranger in a strange land. But he was well aware of his ancestral history.

Don't overlook the fact that Nehemiah was a cupbearer.

Most people think of poison-tasters when they hear that term today, and certainly that was part of Nehemiah's job. But cupbearer was a position of authority in the ancient world. Nehemiah ate every meal at the king's table. He was one of Artaxerxes' primary counselors. He was a leader with power in his own right—an important man in one of the most important kingdoms on the planet.

In short, everything was going well for Nehemiah in spite of his exile. He was living the good life.

And then he heard some news that hit him hard:

> In the month of Kislev in the twentieth year, while I was in the citadel of Susa, Hanani, one of my brothers, came from Judah with some other men, and I questioned them about the Jewish remnant that had survived the exile, and also about Jerusalem.
>
> They said to me, "Those who survived the exile and are back in the province are in great trouble and disgrace. The wall of Jerusalem is broken down, and its gates have been burned with fire."
>
> When I heard these things, I sat down and wept. For some days I mourned and fasted and prayed before the God of heaven. (Nehemiah 1:1–4)

Let's explore what happened next with Nehemiah, the residents of Jerusalem, and the wall around God's city. As we do, I'm going to show you how Nehemiah was driven by his own unique discontent.

More than that, I'm going to show you three practical steps you can take to embrace your unique discontent in a way that contributes to your life and impacts your destiny.

Feel Your Feelings

The first step you can take to embrace your unique discontent is to actively and intentionally feel your feelings.

For many people in our modern culture, feelings are an inconvenience. They are an obstacle that needs to be constantly ignored or shoved aside in order to get things done. Even when we do acknowledge our feelings, it's pretty rare to actually deal with them—to try to understand them or understand what they are revealing about us.

Instead, we shove them down and keep moving forward.

I know it's a stereotype that men are afraid of their feelings or tend to ignore emotions altogether, and there's definitely some truth there in a general sense. But it's not just men. I've worked with many women who viewed their emotions with distaste. They don't like being controlled by those emotions. Again, they might lock themselves in the bathroom for twenty minutes to cry, but that's as far as things go. They don't have a way of processing those feelings that is helpful or constructive.

Look at Nehemiah though. "When I heard these things, I sat down and wept. For some days I mourned and fasted and prayed before the God of heaven" (Nehemiah 1:4).

Later, the text says Nehemiah went to perform his duty at the king's table, but Artaxerxes saw right away that something was wrong:

In the month of Nisan in the twentieth year of King Artaxerxes, when wine was brought for him, I took the wine and gave it to the king. I had not been sad in his presence before, so the king asked me, "Why does your face look so sad when you are not ill? This can be nothing but sadness of heart." (2:1–2)

Nehemiah wasn't afraid of his feelings. He didn't try to bury them or deny them or cover them over with work. Or entertainment. Or pills.

No, he allowed himself to feel his feelings. He sat in them—grief, sadness, frustration, bitterness, and even anger. In fact, he felt those feelings so deeply that even the king noticed something was wrong. The storms raging inside Nehemiah impacted his face and features.

You could say Nehemiah didn't just have strong emotions about the destruction of Jerusalem's wall; those emotions had him. And because Nehemiah paid attention to those emotions, he became aware of his unique discontent.

That's important. Often the first inkling you will have of your unique discontent are the emotions it generates. Maybe you feel frustrated by a specific situation, for example. Or angry. Maybe you feel helpless because you don't have a way to solve a problem—or maybe you feel irritated by the way everyone else seems to ignore that problem. Maybe you're just upset in a way you can't even put into words.

Don't ignore those emotions. Instead, feel them. Sit in them. Explore them. See what they reveal about you—who you are and what you are created to accomplish.

When it comes to your unique discontent, your emotions are like the dashboard lights in your car. It's undoubtedly annoying when one of those lights turns on. *Dang, another problem to solve. More money down the drain. And I just got this paid off too!*

In theory, you could deal with the situation by putting a piece of tape over the dashboard light. That way you won't see it anymore. You won't feel annoyed anymore. Problem solved, right?

Wrong. The light isn't the main issue. It's alerting you to

the fact that something is wrong with your vehicle. By choosing to cover up the light, you're just setting yourself up for a much bigger problem down the road.

The same is true of our emotions. Don't ignore your feelings—especially your feelings of frustration and discontent. Instead, be on the lookout for situations and circumstances that bother you. Pay attention to those emotions. Even embrace them.

But don't stop there!

Do Something

Being aware of your feelings is helpful for identifying and embracing your unique discontent, but there will come a point when awareness is no longer enough.

You need to act.

Let's check back in with Nehemiah. The king noticed something was wrong, and he asked Nehemiah about it. Here's how the cupbearer responded:

> I was very much afraid, but I said to the king, "May the king live forever! Why should my face not look sad when the city where my ancestors are buried lies in ruins, and its gates have been destroyed by fire?"
>
> The king said to me, "What is it you want?"
>
> Then I prayed to the God of heaven, and I answered the king, "If it pleases the king and if your servant has found favor in his sight, let him send me to the city in Judah where my ancestors are buried so that I can rebuild it."
> (2:2–5)

Nehemiah had a chance to take action in a way that could make a real difference, and he didn't put it off. He didn't try to postpone the opportunity or gather a bunch of friends to pray about it for a week.

He seized his chance to do something. "Then I prayed to the God of heaven, and I answered the king" (vv. 4–5). Boom.

But Nehemiah didn't stop there. He asked the king for money, supplies, and permission to rebuild the wall around Jerusalem. Then Nehemiah gathered up an expedition of people and traveled several hundred miles on foot to oversee the construction of that wall himself. I'll spare you the gory details, but Nehemiah pushed and pulled his way through a huge number of obstacles, not just to get the construction started, but to finish it. To see it through to the end.

Scripture says, "So the wall was completed on the twenty-fifth of Elul, in fifty-two days" (6:15). Nehemiah didn't just wallow in his unique discontent; he used his feelings as a driving motivation to get the job done.

I've noticed that many people I serve and coach have trouble getting started when it comes to their own unique discontent—when it comes to the problems they were created to solve. One of the reasons they have trouble is that they don't yet have a plan for fixing the whole problem. They don't know how to make everything better all at once.

In other words, a lot of people do nothing about the issues that drive them crazy because they're waiting for an opportunity to do something huge—something that will fix those issues once and for all.

Unfortunately, most problems don't get solved all at once. Most problems need to be addressed incrementally in order to find a solution. How do you eat an elephant? One bite at a time.

The reality is that embracing your unique discontent in a big way doesn't mean you have to do big things. You can start small. Make a donation. Have a conversation. Volunteer for an hour at a ministry or charity that is addressing the problem you want to solve. Talk about that problem in your church or small group.

Do something.

Here's the principle: *Do what you can until you're able to do what you want.*

Do what you can until you're able to do what you want.

It's okay if you don't have a plan right now for solving global poverty or ending human trafficking around the world. Honestly, that's not realistic. Start smaller. Find what you *can* do right now—right in this moment.

Then do it.

Don't Go Alone

One of the things that resonates with me when I read Nehemiah's story is how good he was at building teams and putting together systems to get things done. These are giftings and passions of mine as well, and it's fun to watch a master at work.

For example, when Nehemiah arrived in Jerusalem, he went out and inspected the ruined city during the middle of the night so he could get a sense of the project in front of him. He examined the walls and the gates. He started to rough out some plans in his mind. But then he gathered the leaders of the city:

Then I said to them, "You see the trouble we are in: Jerusalem lies in ruins, and its gates have been burned with fire. Come, let us rebuild the wall of Jerusalem, and we will no longer be in disgrace." I also told them about the gracious hand of my God on me and what the king had said to me.

They replied, "Let us start rebuilding." So they began this good work. (2:17-18)

Nehemiah could have said, "Here's my letter from the king, which gives me authority over this project. Here's how I want things to go. Now get to work."

Instead, Nehemiah included people in his own story by sharing the ways God had already been at work. He helped the residents of Jerusalem see the trouble they were in—a city with no walls was defenseless against enemy attacks. And then Nehemiah invited the residents of Jerusalem to join his cause. He was a master motivator.

Later, Nehemiah and the residents of Jerusalem faced major trouble from enemies living around Jerusalem—people who didn't want the wall to be rebuilt. Those enemies were so enraged that they made physical threats against Nehemiah and the other builders. Here's how Nehemiah responded:

Therefore I stationed some of the people behind the lowest points of the wall at the exposed places, posting them by families, with their swords, spears and bows. After I looked things over, I stood up and said to the nobles, the officials and the rest of the people, "Don't be afraid of them. Remember the Lord, who is great and awesome, and fight for your families, your sons and your daughters, your wives and your homes."

When our enemies heard that we were aware of their plot and that God had frustrated it, we all returned to the wall, each to our own work.

From that day on, half of my men did the work, while the other half were equipped with spears, shields, bows and armor. The officers posted themselves behind all the people of Judah who were building the wall. Those who carried materials did their work with one hand and held a weapon in the other, and each of the builders wore his sword at his side as he worked. But the man who sounded the trumpet stayed with me. (4:13–18)

Once again, Nehemiah didn't try to solve big problems on his own. Faced with fearful opposition, he rallied his troops and put systems in place that allowed people to defend themselves, even as they kept building. He did everything he could to keep his team both safe and productive, but that meant not doing everything himself. He sought out help.

Then—and I really love this—once the wall was finished, Nehemiah threw a party. He gathered all the people together inside the walls, and they celebrated with food and drink. Not only that, but Nehemiah also asked Ezra the priest to teach the people from God's Law, the Scriptures. This was crucial, because the root cause of Jerusalem's destruction was the people's rejection of God. Their idolatry. Nehemiah wasn't just concerned with raising up physical walls. He also wanted to knock down the spiritual walls that had separated his people from God.

Again, he tackled this project as part of a team. He wasn't an expert in the Scriptures, so he found an expert in the Scriptures to teach people what they needed to know about following God.

Do you sense where I'm going with all this? I know from experience that people can become loners when they try to address the problems that bother them most. I've been there myself. We think the fact that God designed us to tackle a specific issue means we are supposed to tackle it by ourselves.

Not true.

Yes, your unique discontent is specific to you, but that doesn't mean you're supposed to limit the solution to you. Don't go alone. Instead, like Nehemiah, seek out others who can help you make a bigger impact than you are able to make by yourself.

In my experience, that means starting by looking to see where God is already at work. Many of the problems that bother you most really will be too big for you to handle. But that's okay because nothing is too big for God to handle. Look to see where he is already addressing the issues connected with your unique discontent, and then seek out the opportunities he will provide for you to jump on board.

Not going alone also means looking to see where other people are already at work—or looking to find other people who are bothered by the same problems you are trying to solve.

> **Start by looking to see where God is already at work.**

As you have conversations with those close to you, be open about your unique discontent. Talk about your frustrations and your desire to make a difference. Then see whose eyes light up. Listen for people to echo the same feelings you've been dealing with—and then invite them to join you.

You really can contribute to solving the issues and problems that bother you most. But to do that with any sort of success—to both identify and embrace your unique identity—you need to feel your feelings, take action when action is possible, and refuse to go alone.

CHAPTER 3

UNIQUE DREAMS

"Follow your dreams!"

How often have you heard that passionate appeal in recent months? Or maybe something similar, like "Chase your dreams!" "Don't give up on your dreams!" I saw something on social media recently that said, "Follow your dreams; they know the way."

There is a near-universal consensus in our culture that people would be happier, healthier, and way more successful if only they would follow their dreams. Chase their desires. Pursue their passions.

You know what? I agree. I believe our communities in general would be in better shape if all of us were better equipped to identify our dreams and achieve them. I believe each of us as individuals would be more secure in our own skin and our own success if we were supported in chasing that which we were designed to chase. In fact, my thesis for this chapter is that in order to find meaning and purpose through our unique identity, you and I must both understand and pursue our unique dreams.

So, yes, follow your dreams. Pursue your passions.

To a point.

Because just as we saw in chapter 1 with the idea of "be yourself," there are several different ways to go about this concept of chasing your dreams—and not all of them are helpful. Indeed, many of them are harmful.

For most people today—and certainly for society at large—pursuing their dreams means making decisions and living a life that is primarily focused on *their* happiness. *Their* success. *Their* sense of meaning and purpose. Most of us believe that following our dreams is centered on doing whatever benefits us most.

That is not the case.

How do I know? Because we've been chasing our dreams that way for generations now. We've been looking out for number one. We've become experts in self-care. And we've become our own number-one fans. The result of all this emphasis on *me* and *my* is a culture bursting with strife, selfishness, and diseases of despair. The more we have pursued our dreams for our own interests, the more those interests have proved to be unsatisfying.

That's the bad news. The good news is that there is a way to chase your dreams and avoid all that mess. There is a way to pursue your passions that results in genuine fulfillment both for yourself and others.

The key is to ground your pursuit on the foundation of your *unique identity*. Remember, you are different from every other person who has ever lived or ever will live. Your difference is your superpower. You were handcrafted and uniquely designed with a purpose in mind. That purpose was not predicated on your pleasure. You were not created simply so that you as an individual could be healthy, wealthy, and wise.

No, you were created to contribute to the flourishing of humanity as a whole. Your unique identity is a key to unlocking happiness not just for you but for your community and beyond.

When you pursue your passions with that goal in mind—the elevation of yourself *and* others rather than yourself at the *expense* of others—you will experience the power of both chasing and catching what I call *unique dreams*.

THREE CHARACTERISTICS OF OUR DREAMS

As I mentioned earlier, your unique dreams are a key factor when it comes to living out your unique identity in a way that produces meaning and purpose. But first, let's look at what unique dreams are *not*.

Unique dreams are not goals or specific targets in terms of what we hope to achieve or accomplish. That's how our society typically thinks of "dreams," right? They are those hopeful but also probably unrealistic goals we would like to achieve in the distant future. "My dream is to be the CEO of a Fortune 500 company." Or "my dream is to write scripts for Hollywood." Or "my dream is to retire on my own island in the South Pacific."

Those are not the dreams I'm talking about. Those are not your unique dreams. They're more like wishes or career goals—reflections of your current hopes rather than revelations of your identity.

What are unique dreams, then? There are three important characteristics that will help us develop a working definition.

First, *they are more emotive than concrete*. You'll have a better chance of identifying your unique dreams if you examine how you feel more closely than what you want to achieve.

In a lot of ways, your unique dreams function as the inverse of your unique discontent. As I mentioned in the previous chapter, you can identify your unique discontent by paying attention to what exasperates you—what irritates you. That's because the problems that bother you most are likely the problems you were created to solve.

On the flip side, you can identify your unique dreams by paying attention to what excites you—what inspires you. An important word here is *passion*. Our unique dreams often grow out of those situations about which we feel most passionate. Rather than problems that irritate us, unique dreams express themselves as opportunities that grab our attention and cause our eyes to light up with anticipation.

The opportunities that inspire you most are often the opportunities you were created to seize.

Here's how I would verbalize that principle: *the opportunities that inspire you most are often the opportunities you were created to seize.*

Take a moment and consider yourself, including your own feelings and internal feedback. As you move in and out of your community and the world at large, what situations and circumstances wake you up? Make you feel alive? Where do you see opportunities for victory and impact when others just see another setback?

Answering these questions should start to point you in the direction of your unique dreams. But there's still more to unpack.

The second truth about unique dreams is that *they are directly related to unique design.* They are both a connection to and an outgrowth of who you are at the core.

When I was younger, there was not much I was more passionate about than basketball. I had a deep desire to play the game as much as possible, and any adults who asked me about career aspirations invariably got the same answer: "I'm going to the NBA." This was beyond fun or entertainment. I took basketball seriously. I was a student of the game, as they say. I had every intention of becoming the next Michael Jordan and cementing my legacy as a true hero of the sport.

Sadly, there was a critical roadblock to my plans (and my dream) called genetics. As I progressed toward adulthood, it became clear that I would never fill out MJ's six-foot-six frame as a shooting guard. Even as I continued to study and practice with true passion and a genuine desire to improve, it was obvious that I did not possess the physical tools to compete at the highest levels of my favorite sport.

In other words, my passion for basketball did not have a firm connection with my unique design. Not when it came to long-term plans or goals.

Of course, this connection between unique dreams and unique design goes way beyond the physical attributes of your body. It also includes your personality. Your character. Your experiences. Your ambitions. Your connections and relationships. Really, your unique dreams will be an expression of everything that makes you uniquely you.

> **Your unique dreams will be an expression of everything that makes you uniquely you.**

One of the things I've learned about myself is that I have no problem being mobile. I've lived in a bunch of different places up and down the United States, and I don't look back on our different geographical moves as a problem or a hindrance. Instead, they have been opportunities to experience new people and new places. The same is true for short-term travel. I like the privilege of being on the go and engaging with new cultures and communities on a regular basis.

Looking back over my life, I can see that my mobility has been an important factor in my own passionate pursuit of my unique dreams. That mobility has allowed me to plant and lead transformational communities not just in my hometown but also around the world.

The same will be true of you. The plan and purpose that went into your unique design will highlight and support your pursuit of your unique dreams.

The third truth about unique dreams—which I alluded to above—is that *they will help you achieve a unique impact in the world*. Your unique dreams won't be just about you and your goals and your success. Rather, they will contribute to human flourishing in a broader way. They will help you make your ultimate contribution in the world, which is a topic we're going to explore in more depth in chapter 4 when we talk about *unique destiny*.

MYRON'S STORY

Myron Rolle is one of the most interesting human beings on this planet, and I continue to be amazed that his story is not better known. If you've never heard of him, Myron is an All-American football player who starred at Florida State University and was drafted by the Tennessee Titans of the National Football League. (He played for the Pittsburgh Steelers as well.) And Myron is an intellectual giant who was awarded a Rhodes Scholarship to study medicine at Oxford University, did his residency at Harvard Medical School, and is now a leading neurosurgeon who practices at his own clinic.

In other words, Myron Rolle has been an unqualified success in two of the world's most difficult fields to participate in, let alone dominate. He's basically a superhero. He's also a fantastic example of what it looks like to identify and pursue unique dreams.

Let me offer a little backstory so you can see what I mean.

All the way back in fifth grade, Myron knew he wanted to be a doctor. He was passionate about helping people, and he caught a spark when he read the book *Gifted Hands* by Dr. Ben Carson—a Black neurosurgeon who later became a model in Myron's life. Obviously, any fifth grader who reads medical autobiographies is a different kind of kid. Thankfully, Myron's family considered his difference to be a blessing rather than a curse.

As he continued to grow, Myron also excelled in sports. By his senior year of high school, he was the top-ranked football recruit in the nation, dominating the competition both as a running back and on defense. When he signed to play for Florida State, boosters and fans alike were elated.

It was there, at Florida State, that Myron started to feel some real pressure about picking a side. Choosing a lane.

He excelled academically, earning his bachelor's degree in just two and a half years. But even with his success, he noticed that a lot of people questioned his decisions. Why did he keep playing football when he obviously had such a promising future in medicine? Why spend his time chasing after leather balls when he could dedicate himself to saving lives? Wasn't it time to grow up and stop playing games?

The pressure from the athletic side was more intense. During his years as a Seminole, Myron excelled in every way as a performer and leader on the football team. He was an All-American tackling machine with a nose for making plays. He won awards even as the team won game after game. He was an exemplary role model both on the field and in the locker room.

Yet from the beginning there were many who questioned Myron's dedication to football. What started as subtle whispers eventually became shouts. People wondered if his academic workload left him enough time for film study every week. They worried his commitment to charitable causes would hinder his commitment to the team.

Basically, Myron was living in two worlds, and both of those worlds were pushing him to leave the other. Both worlds were pushing him to conform to *their* expectations for his present and his future. They wanted Myron to make an either-or choice when it came to which dreams he should pursue.

Thankfully, Myron had a solid understanding of who he was at the core and what he wanted to accomplish. He was aware of his *unique identity*. And that awareness allowed him to reject the either-or opinions of outsiders and instead embrace a both-and mentality as he pursued his *unique dreams*.

The best example of that pursuit came on November 22, 2008—the day Florida State was scheduled to play the University of Maryland at College Park. A big game near the end of a big season.

Then Myron got some news. He had been named a finalist for the prestigious Rhodes Scholarship, which was a huge deal. There are only thirty-two Americans who become Rhodes Scholars every year, earning the chance to study for a degree at Oxford University in England. Myron was on the short list. He just needed to sit for one final interview to complete the application process.

Can you guess when that interview was supposed to take place? Yep, November 22. The same day as the big football game against Maryland.

Once again, Myron had people who were pushing him to pick a lane. Many said, "This is one of the biggest games of the year. If you bail on your team right now, you'll blow your chance at playing in the NFL." Others told him: "Becoming a Rhodes Scholar is a once-in-a-lifetime opportunity. Don't blow it because of some stupid game."

Once again, Myron rejected the pressure to conform to the either-or expectations of others. Instead, he embraced his unique dreams and reached for both-and.

That meant Myron spent the week prior to November 22 both practicing with the team and studying hard. When Saturday came, he was in Birmingham, Alabama, for the Rhodes Scholarship interview. It was a grueling two hours, and then Myron waited for another hour before hearing the results. He was in! He'd been accepted to the program! But he wasn't finished. He hopped on a plane to Maryland and arrived at the stadium near the beginning of the second quarter. Myron and the rest of the Seminoles defense held Maryland's offense to just three points en route to a 37–3 victory.[1]

Talk about both-and! Myron Rolle was laser-focused on remaining true to his unique identity and pursuing his unique dreams.

One last point on this story, and it's an important one: pursuing your unique dreams almost always comes with a cost. There is a price to pay for rejecting conformity. Sometimes that price is relational, such as when people attack or abandon us because we refuse to accommodate their expectations. Other times the price includes lost opportunities, lost respect, lost sleep, and more.

For Myron Rolle, the cost of pursuing his unique dreams was financial—at least at the beginning. Remember the Rhodes Scholarship? That meant moving overseas to study at Oxford for a year, which Myron was eager to do. The issue was that Myron was one of the best college football players in the country and was expected to enter the NFL draft. Most analysts believed he would be chosen in the first round, which would have guaranteed him a four- or five-year contract worth more than ten million dollars.

Pursuing your unique dreams almost always comes with a cost.

In spite of such gaudy numbers, Myron skipped the 2008 NFL draft. He went to Oxford. While there, he kept his daily practice of working out at 5:00 a.m. in order to stay physically ready for the rigors of the NFL. Then in 2009, Myron rejoined the NFL draft and was selected by the Tennessee Titans in the sixth round.

I remember there were a lot of sportswriters that year talking about Myron Rolle's "mistake." As they predicted, skipping a year of football had severely impacted Myron's draft status and subsequent contract. He really did forfeit millions of dollars by participating in the Rhodes Scholarship program.

But none of those decisions were mistakes from Myron's point of view, because Myron had a both-and mindset. That was his identity, and embracing both opportunities was his unique dream.

These days, Myron Rolle is still pursuing those dreams. In fact, he finds himself in the unique position of examining the effects of traumatic brain injuries from physical sports—such as football—from the dual perspective of a neurosurgeon and a retired NFL player.

Which means he is exactly where he was created to be and doing exactly what he was created to do.

Would you like to say the same thing about yourself today?

Or a year from now? Or ten years? Then let's keep digging. Specifically, let's see how the passionate pursuit of our unique dreams plays out in everyday life.

LIVING OUT OUR DREAMS

As a reminder, the concept of unique dreams can be difficult to quantify because those dreams are rarely connected to concrete goals or achievements. We're not talking about the top three entries on your bucket list.

Also, every person's experience with identifying and living out their unique dreams will be different from the experiences of others—because unique dreams are unique. You will not have the same dreams as me, and neither of us will have the same specific dreams and passions as those around us. Each of us needs to approach our dreams as opportunities to flesh out and act on our unique identity.

Still, there are some common pathways we can follow to explore the practical applications of our unique dreams on a deeper level. As we saw earlier, unique dreams typically follow three important characteristics:

1. They are more emotive than concrete, being connected to those situations and circumstances that inspire us and make us feel genuinely alive.
2. They are directly related to our unique design, which means we will be specifically equipped and prepared to pursue them. If we are chasing passions that have no connection to the way we were designed, it's likely those passions are distractions rather than central to our purpose.

3. They are not wishes based on pleasing ourselves; rather, unique dreams are passions that help us contribute to human flourishing as a whole.

You can use these three characteristics as guardrails to start the process of identifying your own unique dreams.

But what about real life? What about the situations we experience and the choices we make each day? What do unique dreams look like on a more practical level? Those are critical questions. Our deepest dreams and passions don't just exist "out there" in some theoretical future; they impact our lives right here. Right now.

In my own life—and in my experiences in recent decades as a pastor, coach, and mentor—I've observed that our unique dreams typically get lived out in three distinct stages: calling, roles, and expressions. Let's explore each of those stages in a little more depth.

Our Calling

As I mentioned earlier, all people are intended to contribute to human flourishing for all people. Every human being has been specially and specifically designed to advance the cause of all human beings. We know this is true because we are not random byproducts of an uncaring universe.

No, each of us was created for a purpose. You. Me. All of us.

But we don't all have the same purpose. We're not supposed to contribute to human flourishing in the same way. Because each of us is unique, we have unique dreams and unique ways to make an impact in the world. And that impact begins with "calling."

That's a word we use a lot in our culture, and we typically use it vaguely. "I have a calling to help people." Or "I feel called to the ministry." We often fail to realize that a calling can't drop out of the sky. A calling requires a caller. In our case, it requires a Creator.

With that in mind, here's how I define calling: *God's invitation for your participation and the reason for your creation.*

First, your calling is an *invitation* from your Creator. When you feel nudged or pulled toward a specific work or when you develop a passion to serve in a specific way, this is your Creator reaching out to show you *how* he made you—to show you *why* he made you. He is inviting you to fulfill your purpose.

Second, God is calling you for the reason of *participation*, not rumination. Too many people like to think about their calling or meditate on their purpose. But these kinds of mental games don't accomplish anything for us or for our communities. The only time we participate in our calling is when we act. The only time we participate in human flourishing is when we do something that contributes to human flourishing.

More than that, your calling is God's invitation to participate in what he is already doing. Remember, God is at work in this world. God is at work in your community. And he has given you a calling as an invitation to join his efforts. Therefore, following your calling means aligning your life with what God wants to do through you and around you.

Finally, your calling is directly related to the *reason* for your creation. It is directly connected to your purpose. Your mission. Your raison d'être. Your calling doesn't apply to whims or superficial wants. It's tied to who you are at the core—to your *unique identity*.

After college, I planned on attending law school and becoming a lawyer. I don't remember all the reasons I chose that route for myself, but there were plenty of good reasons. I wanted to help people and I wanted to be successful, and a legal career seemed like a good option for achieving both of those goals.

Over time, though, I began to feel strongly that God was pulling me off that path. I felt it internally through my own convictions and my own interactions with God's Spirit, and I felt it externally in the conversations I had with others I respected.

Eventually, I realized that God was calling me—inviting me—into pastoral ministry. He was showing me the reason for my creation. Having followed that calling for decades now, I have a much better understanding of my calling. Specifically, I am called to launch and lead transformational communities around the world.

What about you? How would you describe your calling? Where is God specifically inviting you to join his work in your community and beyond?

Our Roles

As you've noticed by now, the way I am describing *calling* is fairly general. Or broad. You might even say vague. That's because your calling is a direction more than a destination. As we just saw, it's responding to God's invitation and aligning with his work in a way that is directly connected to who you are.

Once you begin moving in the direction of your calling, you will find opportunities to carry out that calling through different *roles*. Here's how I define these roles: *specific responsibilities God gives a person for specific seasons.*

You can think of a role as a job title. Let's say an individual has a calling to improve the lives of children, for example. There are a wide variety of roles that will allow that individual to live out their calling through their everyday life: teacher, social worker, foster parent, coach, pediatrician, entertainer, and so on. Each of those roles is connected to the overall calling of serving and blessing children.

Now, am I saying these roles will always be paying jobs that pertain to your career? No. The roles you fulfill as you live out your calling can include volunteer opportunities, internships, unpaid positions, or just moments when you find yourself in the right place at the right time to make a difference. They also can, and often do, include the kind of work that pays your bills and supports your family.

There are a few other clarifications I want to make about these roles, so let's tackle them one at a time.

First, I've observed in my work as a mentor and a coach that people often confuse their *role* with their *calling*. To say it another way, people often believe the current specific responsibility they are carrying out is the larger reason for their creation—their mission or purpose. In my experience, this is a confusing and often destructive mistake.

Here's an example of how this can occur. Let's say a woman feels called to improve the lives of children, as I mentioned above. She feels that pull—that invitation from her Creator. She has a passion for young people, and she truly comes alive when she has opportunities to live out that passion. For those reasons and more, she takes a job as an elementary school teacher.

The correct way to view this situation is that the woman has a calling to improve the lives of children and she is currently living out that calling through the role of teacher. That's the healthy way of defining and prioritizing her calling and her role.

But things can get switched around if this woman believes she is *called* to be a teacher. She confuses her role with her calling. In that situation, she may cling to that role even long after it makes sense for her to do so. When other opportunities arise—other roles that would allow her to expand or deepen her calling, such as being promoted to school principal or even moving into another career—she may resist these opportunities out of fear. *I can't stop being a teacher. I have to stay true to my calling.*

Remember, role supports your calling, not the other way around.

Actually, I should say *roles*, plural, because most of us have more than one. That's another key point. There are times when we need to change roles in pursuit of our calling—moving from teacher to principal, for example—but there are also times when we need to *add* new or supplementary roles to deepen our calling.

> **Role supports your calling, not the other way around.**

Let's go back to the example of our friend the teacher. She has a calling to improve the lives of children, and she's been focusing on the children in her community by working as a teacher. That's a primary role in her life. But there are other ways she can live out her calling. She could take on the role of "content creator" by writing children's books, posting educational videos on YouTube, or creating instructional content that helps and supports other teachers. She can add an additional role (or several roles) without giving up her job as a teacher.

The point is that there are a lot of active, intentional steps you can take to live out your calling every day.

One more clarification—or maybe this is a warning. There will be times when God places you in roles that seem to make little or no sense. There will be times when God places you in roles that frustrate you. Or confuse you. Or make you angry.

Don't assume you are off target in those moments. Don't assume you have wandered away from your calling. Instead, know that God often uses temporary roles in our lives as a way of changing us and growing us so we can more effectively fulfill our calling.

Let's recap what we've covered so far. All of us are designed to contribute to human flourishing in our world. Our purpose is part of our DNA. We aren't expected to make an impact in the world through random luck; instead, our Creator has given each of us a calling—an invitation to participate in what he is doing. Then we live out our calling through different roles, which are specific functions and responsibilities we carry out for specific periods of time. Sometimes we just have a single role in support of our calling, moving from one to another when the timing is right. Often we fulfill several roles at the same time.

Our Expressions

The final category through which we live out our calling is what I refer to as *expressions*. Here's how I define this idea: an expression is *the working out of an individual's personality and preferences while doing work.*

To say it another way, expressions are the ways we carry out our roles based on our unique identity. Let me give you an example of what this looks like in real life. Earlier we talked about "teacher" as a role that people can take on as they live out their calling. I know a lot of teachers, but there are two specific individuals who come to mind.

The first is a guy named Mark, who has been an educator for a long time. He's a high school teacher and a complete professional. He knows how to present information in a way that is clear and concise, and he does a wonderful job of teaching that information to young people through what we might call "traditional" methods. He stands up in front of the class, explains the concepts, gives examples, answers questions, reinforces through quizzes and tests, and so on. He is a wonderful teacher who gets wonderful results.

Then there's another guy in my church named CJ Reynolds. He teaches high school literature in West Philadelphia. If you want to check him out, he's got a YouTube channel called "Real Rap with Reynolds!"—and you'll see from the first video that CJ is anything but traditional or conventional.[2] He uses music and video and artistic expression to help engage young people in a way most of them have never experienced. And not just kids. CJ has expanded his video library to include instructional videos for other teachers. So he's helping other educators learn new and different techniques for teaching.

What I love is that here we have two men who are both carrying out the same role in pursuit of basically the same calling. They are both working to elevate the lives of students through the role of "teacher." Yet their expressions of that role are completely different. Completely unique. Because each man is living out of his unique identity.

Notice I'm not saying CJ is better or more revolutionary than Mark or anything like that. I'm not implying that "different" means "improved."

Instead, I want to hold up both men as examples of individuals whose unique personalities, preferences, and experiences led them to completely different expressions of the same role. Both of those expressions are effective and beneficial to both their calling and to overall human flourishing.

Also, importantly, both men are demonstrating true courage by living out of their unique design, rather than simply conforming to what others are doing.

It's on this level—the expressions we adopt in carrying out our roles—that the uniqueness of our unique dreams really comes into play. As you live and work each day, you will probably find yourself around a lot of people who share a calling that is similar to yours. If you're in a profession where you have regular contact with others who have the same job title as you have, that means you're also going to be in contact with people who have the same role as you have.

But hear me on this, nobody will have the same expressions as you. Nobody can live out your roles in the same way as you live them out, because nobody else has your unique combination of personality, preferences, priorities, and experiences. Nobody else is you.

Here's a principle: *you'll know you've started to catch hold of your unique dreams when you can pursue those dreams and still be true to your unique identity.*

Speaking of which, are you starting to get a sense of your unique dreams? Those passions that have always been part of you? Those pursuits that wake you up and make you feel alive? Those expressions of your calling that speak to who you are way down at the core?

I hope so. Because identifying and pursuing these unique dreams are crucial steps in living the abundant life of meaning and purpose you were created to experience.

GIVE YOURSELF PERMISSION TO GO

There will be obstacles in your life that have the potential to block you from pursuing your unique dreams. Some of these obstacles are part of the ups and downs of regular life. We can run up against any number of challenges that hinder our ability to pursue our unique dreams. Financial challenges. Relational challenges. Health challenges. Emotional challenges. This world can be a difficult place.

Other obstacles are more targeted. More intentional. Remember, just as you have a Creator who has designed you with a specific purpose and unique dreams, you also have an enemy who wants nothing more than to drag you away from that purpose and those dreams. As the apostle Paul wrote, "Our struggle is not against flesh and blood, but against the rulers, against the authorities, against the powers of this dark world and against the spiritual forces of evil in the heavenly realms" (Ephesians 6:12).

As I say, both of these types of obstacles can hinder us from identifying and pursuing our unique dreams. Both of these types of obstacles need to be looked out for and overcome.

But please hear me: *the most significant obstacle between your current life and your unique dreams just might be you.*

What do I mean? Simply that pursuing our dreams can be scary. It can be difficult. It's often costly. And those realities can conspire to convince us that keeping our dreams on the shelf is the best option for now.

Let's not sugarcoat it. There's a lot of work that goes into knowing ourselves well enough to separate our true passions from selfish desires or superficial whims. It takes a lot of reflection to sort out the difference between what we were made to achieve and what others expect us to achieve. Many people simply choose not to attempt that work. *Too difficult,* they conclude.

Beyond that, it takes a lot of investment to pursue our passions and chase our unique dreams. We have to invest the kinds of resources that are hard to acquire and hard to let go of—money, yes, but also time, physical energy, and emotional strength. Many people prefer to avoid these kinds of invest-ments. It's much easier, and much cheaper, to focus on enter-taining ourselves.

Finally, there is the ever-present reality that pursuing our unique dreams doesn't automatically mean we will achieve or realize those dreams. We might fail. We might invest ourselves heavily and passionately—and still fall short. Many people aren't willing to take that risk. The fear of failure is real, and it really impacts our decisions.

For those reasons and more, it's easy to consign our unique dreams to the same shelf as our unrealistic goals. *Once I'm wealthy, I'll start chasing that dream. Once the kids are out of the house, I'll start pursuing that passion. Once I hit retirement age, I'll start thinking about my legacy.*

These are dangerous thoughts. Dangerous waters. Because dreams and complacency are like oil and water—they don't mix.

What about you? What passions have you been pushing down because they're not popular? What pursuits have you been avoiding because they're not predictable? What dreams are you avoiding because they don't seem proper?

Let me challenge you right here and now to give yourself permission not only to identify your unique dreams but to pursue them. Give yourself permission to go.

Yes, it may be scary. Go anyway. Yes, it may cost you some-thing—it may even cost you everything. Go anyway. Yes, you may fail and miss out on what you *think* is the purpose for your life, but go anyway. Because if you stay on the couch, you will *certainly* miss out.

Give yourself permission to pursue your unique dreams. Chase them. Let yourself feel that life and vitality. Let yourself believe you can achieve what God designed you to achieve. And then go. Get moving. Take action.

CHAPTER 4

YOUR UNIQUE DESTINY

In May 2011, a man named James Harrison walked into a Red Cross donation center in his native Australia. The receptionist greeted him by name, and Harrison took his place in the waiting room with practiced ease. No apprehension for the coming needle. No nervousness.

When the technician called out his name, Harrison walked through familiar hallways and sat down in a familiar chair. His sleeve was already rolled up. Ready for business. After smelling the brief odor of rubbing alcohol and feeling the quick, cold touch of a sterilizing wipe, Harrison looked away as the technician inserted the needle.

I assume that was his least favorite part of the experience.

People who donate blood and plasma benefit their communities in many ways, which is why many people are donors. It's a wonderful thing when people literally give of themselves in order to help others. Even to save lives.

But James Harrison's donations are a little different—actually, they are *a lot* different. Let me quickly explain.

Way back in 1951, when Harrison was fourteen years old, he was forced to undergo major chest surgery. It was an emergency, and the young Harrison was able to survive the surgery only because others had donated blood—he used more than two units of blood during his recovery. Those donations saved Harrison's life. As a result, he resolved to be a blood donor and do his part to return the favor.

Here's where things get interesting. After a few donations, doctors realized Harrison's blood contained an incredibly important—and incredibly rare—antibody called anti-RhD, which is necessary for treating a dangerous condition called rhesus disease (Rh disease). Most mothers know that term, but for all the dads reading this, Rh disease afflicts children while they are still in the womb. When a mother's blood is RhD-negative but the baby's blood is RhD-positive (inherited from the father), the mother's body will perceive the baby as a foreign object and attack it.

In most cases, Rh disease will result in serious brain damage or death for the infant—unless treated. How is it treated? By giving the mother a treatment called anti-D immune globulin, which contains the necessary anti-D antibody.

Back to James Harrison. As I said, doctors quickly noticed that Harrison's blood contained high concentrations of the antibody. They didn't understand why or how that could be, but they did understand that Harrison's plasma would literally be a lifesaver. So they made sure to explain the situation to young James.

Young James responded by donating plasma instead of blood to maximize the amount of anti-D antibody collected. Then he donated again. And again. And again.

Back to that Red Cross donation center in May 2011. On that day, James Harrison walked into his regular clinic once again, greeted the technician by name once again, endured the sting of the needle yet again—all in order to give his one thousandth donation of plasma.

I know one thousand is a round number, but stop to think about it for a moment. You can only donate plasma every three weeks, which means any person can donate a maximum of seventeen times per year. James Harrison started donating plasma in 1954. To reach his one thousandth donation, he returned faithfully every three weeks *for almost sixty years*! And he wasn't finished. He gave his final donation in 2018, and he only stopped because Australian law prevents people from donating blood or plasma once they turn eighty-one.

According to Jemma Falkenmire of the Australian Red Cross Blood Service, "Every batch of Anti-D that has ever been made in Australia has come from James' blood."[1] Even more impressive, doctors estimate Harrison's donations have saved the lives of nearly 2.5 million unborn children.

Talk about contributing to human flourishing!

Harrison himself is pretty chill about his own generosity. "I'm in a safe room, donating blood. They give me a cup of coffee and something to nibble on," he said.[2] "It's something I can do. It's one of my talents—probably my only talent is that I can be a blood donor."[3]

James Harrison has rightly won numerous awards for his contributions to society, including a prestigious honor called the Medal of the Order of Australia. He even has his own page in the *Guinness World Records*—for the most blood donated by one person.

But what I want to point out is that regardless of the accolades, James Harrison has made an impact. He has improved his community, but not just his community. He has enriched his country, but not just his country. James Harrison has literally changed the world.

For that reason, he is a wonderful illustration of what it means not only to pursue your *unique dreams* but to achieve your *unique destiny*.

YOUR DIFFERENCE IS THE BEST DIFFERENCE

One of the things I like most about James Harrison's story is the way the story was programmed and predetermined even before his birth. Long before the doctors or Harrison himself were aware of the special properties of his plasma, those properties were preparing him to make an impact. To change lives.

For James Harrison, his difference is in his DNA. Literally, it's in his blood. It's part of who he is at the very core.

But here's the principle I have been hammering throughout this book: the same is true for you and me.

Each of us has been handcrafted by our Creator with a *unique design*. We have been intentionally shaped by a specific set of character traits, physical traits, talents, and experiences. Because of our unique design, each of us interacts with the world in a distinctive way, which often causes us to feel a *unique discontent*. Certain issues and circumstances bother us more than they bother other people—which is a good thing, because the problems that irritate us most are likely the problems we were created to solve. At the same time, each of us carries the responsibility to pursue our *unique dreams*, which are those situations or circumstances that inspire us or make us feel alive. Why? Because the opportunities that inspire us most are often the opportunities we were created to seize.

All of this is wrapped up in what I call *unique identity*. The more we understand the power of our design, the more we will allow our discontent and dreams to shape the course of our lives and direct us toward our specific purpose. The more we will be blessed with meaning and fulfillment. And in the words of Jesus, the more we will experience abundant life (John 10:10).

Unique destiny is the pinnacle of that process in your life. To give a definition, *your unique destiny is your ultimate contribution to human flourishing.*

To go back to James Harrison, I imagine he has done a lot of interesting and important things with his eighty-plus years on this planet. He started a family. He had a career. He's a key figure in his community. He has contributed to the world in many ways. But his *ultimate* contribution is his decades-long faithfulness in giving of himself in order to save the lives of millions of unborn children. That is James Harrison's unique destiny.

> Your unique destiny is your ultimate contribution to human flourishing.

When you look through the pages of history, the people who stand out tallest are often those who achieved their unique destiny—their specific and ultimate contribution to human flourishing. Think of Rosa Parks, who not only refused to leave her seat on a public bus but also served as an important figure in the Montgomery bus boycott, which itself became a key moment in the movement for civil rights. That was her unique destiny, and she embraced it.

Think of Candy Lightner, whose thirteen-year-old daughter was killed by a drunk driver—not just a drunk driver, but a repeat offender. Lightner pushed through her grief and rage to found MADD (Mothers Against Drunk Driving) in 1980. Her organization has raised awareness about the dangers of driving while intoxicated and helped pass numerous laws against drunk driving on both the state and federal levels. Her ultimate contribution has included both saving the lives of the innocent and helping those who need to break the power of addiction.

Think of Elon Musk. As an entrepreneur, Musk has already been incredibly successful—having become the world's richest person.[4] He launched SpaceX and Tesla, among several other companies. But those aren't his ultimate contributions—not according to Musk himself. He views his ultimate destiny as helping humanity literally reach for the stars by first populating other planets within our solar system and then continuing to move outward. Even as I write this, SpaceX recently announced plans for a new vehicle called "Starship" that will be capable of transporting up to a hundred people to Mars.[5]

These are all examples of people reaching for and achieving their unique destinies. But there are millions more. Billions. Every human being has the potential to reach for and achieve their unique destiny.

That doesn't mean every human being has the opportunity to be a celebrity. Or rich. Or remembered in the history books. Or even Instagram-famous. That's not what I'm saying. What I am saying is that every person—no matter their background or life experiences or obstacles that have held them back—has the opportunity to contribute to human flourishing in a major way.

Including you. And me.

The language I've been using throughout this book is that I need to think in terms of making *my* difference rather than *a* difference. You need to focus your attention on making *your* difference in this world.

A lot of people want to make a difference, but only in a

generic sense. A lot of people are seeking to have an impact in their communities, but it isn't measurable in any meaningful way. Settling for a vague idea of "doing something good with my life" is just that—settling. We were created to strive for more. We are destined to do better.

When you set your sights on achieving *your* difference in your community and your world—the difference you, specifically, were designed to make—you will be on the right path to seizing your unique destiny.

Let me offer a couple more clarifications before we jump to the next section.

First, your unique destiny is the ultimate contribution you were designed to make in this world, but it's *not your only contribution*. I'm not saying you and I have only one shot to achieve anything worthwhile through our lives. Not at all. Each and every day is bursting with opportunities for us to make a meaningful contribution to human flourishing simply by living out of who we are.

Second, your unique destiny is the ultimate contribution you were designed to make, but it's *not the only contribution that matters*, the only contribution that is significant or weighty. I want to be careful here because it could be easy for you to hear me saying that your unique destiny will be something big and momentous, while the rest of your life will be small and insignificant.

I'm not saying that. Not at all.

Remember, your difference is your superpower, your X factor. You were handcrafted by the all-knowing Creator of the universe—you were specially and specifically designed by God, who says you are created in his image. Remember Prometheus from Greek mythology? He was the one who stole fire from the gods and gave it as a gift to humanity. Well, like

Prometheus, you have been blessed to carry the spark of something more powerful than you or I will ever understand.

For all those reasons and more, you have every opportunity to leverage your unique identity in a way that matters—in a way that is truly significant. This is true before, during, and after that season where you achieve your unique destiny.

PERMISSION TO BE PATIENT

Speaking of making a difference, I want to take an opportunity to say something right now that I hope will bring freedom to your life, lift a burden off your shoulders, and help balance your expectations.

Here it is: *it's okay if you're not making your ultimate contribution in this current season of your life.*

Maybe you're getting up early every morning to drag yourself to a job that is just a job. You don't really want to be there, but you need to be there. People are depending on you. Still, you know there's going to be a moment tomorrow morning when you seriously consider chucking that alarm clock out the window and staying in bed. You don't see any chance to do anything significant right now. You're just trying to make it through each day.

You know what? That's okay.

Maybe you're inundated every day by children—not to mention all the accoutrements that come with children. You've got meals to make. You've got playdates to plan. You've got stories to read and boo-boos to bandage. And none of it ever stops! There's never a break! You have hopes and plans for the future, but right now all your time and energy need to be funneled into those little ones who need you constantly.

That's okay too.

Maybe you were right in the middle of pursuing your unique dreams and stretching out toward your unique destiny, but there's been a hitch. You've been derailed in some way. The doctor called and said, "I've got bad news." Or your boss called you into the corner office and said those same four words. Or any number of unplanned problems that have the potential to break your momentum and knock you back three steps just when you thought you were ready to break through.

Again, that's okay.

It's okay if you haven't yet achieved your unique destiny, and it's okay if your season of life right now can be described by adjectives such as *steady, tedious, ordinary,* or even *boring.*

Why do I mention that? Because I've noticed an increasing pressure in today's culture to expect constant contribution. Constant impact. Constant success. As a society, our dreams have never been bigger and our expectations never higher. That's not necessarily a bad thing. But we need to be careful to keep our sense of perspective in terms of what is realistic and what is achievable.

I was talking recently with a nineteen-year-old young man who is a good kid. Smart. Strong. Handsome. The world is his oyster. But he looked at me with a straight face and said, "I feel like I'm wasting my life."

My first thought was, *You're in college! You haven't even really started your life.*

But I didn't say that, because I understood the pressure he was feeling both internally and externally. At his age, he already expected himself to be a key cog in an organization or a movement that was changing the world. He already expected himself to be a financial success. He already expected himself not simply to be recognized by society at large but to be an influential voice that millions would hear and follow.

Simon Sinek addressed those expectations in a well-known video on the subject of younger workers:

> It's as if they are standing at the foot of a mountain, and they have this abstract concept called "impact" that they want to have on the world, which is the summit. What they don't see is the mountain. I don't care if you go up the mountain quickly or slowly, but there's still a mountain.
>
> And so what this young generation needs to learn is patience. That some things that really, really matter—like love or job fulfillment, joy, love of life, self-confidence, a skill set, any of these things—all of these things take time. Sometimes you can expedite pieces of it, but the overall journey is arduous and long and difficult, and if you don't ask for help and learn that skill set, you will fall off the mountain.[6]

I like that visual. It's helpful to think of your unique destiny as the top of a mountain, and your life as part of the journey toward that summit. I say "part of the journey" because your life doesn't end once you make your ultimate contribution. Sometimes you have other mountains to climb, and sometimes you have wonderful opportunities to help others reach their summits.

Regardless of what imagery we use, the reality is that your unique destiny will likely be connected to a specific season of your life during which you will be most fruitful and most productive. Moreover, you won't reach that season—that summit— simply by getting older. Making your ultimate contribution requires years (probably decades) of hard work. It requires preparation. It requires failure and learning from failure. It is the culmination of recognizing your *unique design*, responding to your *unique discontent*, and reaching for your *unique dreams*.

Please note that we see this principle operating in just about every area of life and we accept it. Look at the natural world, for example. Just because a fruit tree is a fruit tree doesn't mean it will produce fruit. That tree needs to be planted in the right conditions in order to thrive. It needs time to physically grow. And even when it starts to produce fruit, the first several harvests are often small. Only when that tree reaches full maturity will it produce an abundance of produce.

Look at our sports heroes for another example. As I was growing up, Michael Jordan was my idol. Yet it's a well-known story that MJ—the greatest basketball player of all time, in my humble opinion—did not make the varsity team during his sophomore year of high school. He had to play on the JV team. Why? Because he hadn't yet reached a level of physical or emotional maturity that made it appropriate for him to advance.

Even after Jordan achieved stardom in the NBA, he didn't sustain his level of elite success indefinitely. Jordan and the Chicago Bulls won six championships, which was an awesome run. I remember it fondly. But remember when Jordan came out of retirement to play for the Washington Wizards? That wasn't so pretty. He had already made his ultimate contribution to the sport, and he had entered a different season as an athlete.

Or look at the way businesses operate in the world today. Steve Jobs and Steve Wozniak founded Apple in 1976. They were successful in many ways, and certainly the company had several notable moments. But it wasn't until the release of the iPod in 2001 that Apple the company became Apple the movement. The company had to grow and work through obstacles before it reached a season of making its ultimate contribution.

Do you remember that season, by the way? It was crazy! First the iPod. Then the iPhone. Then the iPad. Each year, it seemed like Apple wasn't just releasing a new product; they were revolutionizing our lives.

What about today, though? When I look around, I don't see people waiting in long lines outside the Apple Store each time a new iPhone is released. That season of ultimate contribution has passed, and Apple is back to being "only" a tremendously successful corporation.

The point I'm trying to make here is that you need to give yourself permission to be patient when it comes to your unique destiny. Just because you are not currently making your ultimate contribution to human flourishing doesn't mean anything is wrong. It doesn't mean you're failing. It doesn't mean you're wasting your life.

More than likely, it simply means you are growing, learning, striving, adapting, trying, working, revising, and moving yourself forward.

LIVING YOUR SWEET SPOT

I want to reiterate two primary ideas. The first is that every human being created by God has been programmed with the ability and opportunity to contribute to human flourishing in a major way. Every individual has the ability to achieve their ultimate destiny.

Actually, it's not simply that we have the *ability* to reach our ultimate destiny; it's that we were created for that specific purpose. Which means we carry the *responsibility* to make our ultimate contribution to human flourishing.

That includes me, you, and everyone.

The second idea is that reaching my ultimate destiny will likely mean achieving a season in my life where I am highly productive and effective, which will enable me to make my ultimate contribution in the world—the impact I alone have been created to achieve. I say "season" because that's what it is—a temporary period. An extended moment. Most of us don't reach the point of making our ultimate contribution early in life, and most of us don't maintain that ultimate contribution through years or decades.

Living in your unique destiny means living through a period of life where everything clicks and you are able to make *your* difference in the world naturally and confidently rather than settling for something generic.

I once had a conversation with a fellow pastor who said, "Dharius, I feel like I'm Lebroning right now." He must have seen the confused look on my face, because he explained, "I've been a pastor for twenty years, so I've got my feet under me to the point where I know what I'm doing. But I'm still young enough that I have the energy to do it."

What he called Lebroning is a great picture of living in the season I call your ultimate destiny.[7]

Now comes the big question. *If I'm not ready to make my ultimate contribution—if I'm not on the verge of reaching my unique destiny—what should I do? What's next?*

Let's imagine you're a young person who has big dreams but not a lot of experience. Am I saying you should press pause on those dreams for ten or twenty years? Am I saying you should dive into video games or social media because you don't have a chance to achieve anything meaningful right now? Am I saying you should just concentrate on yourself and your own needs because you don't really have a chance to make a difference in the world during your current season?

Nope. I'm not saying any of that.

Or let's imagine you are a little older—middle age or beyond. You've had some ups and downs, but you've not approached anything that sounds like your unique destiny or your ultimate contribution. Am I saying the window has closed? Am I saying life has passed you by and it's up to younger generations to take up the cause and make an impact? Am I saying you should resign yourself to a few more years of mediocrity before it's time to retire and concentrate on the fishing scene in Florida?

Nope. Not saying any of that either.

Remember, your unique destiny is your ultimate contribution to human flourishing, but it's not your *only* contribution—nor is it your only contribution that matters. When you live out of your unique identity, you will have opportunities to make your difference every day of the week.

Now here's a principle we need to hold close no matter what season of life we're in: *Everything we sow in the present has a direct influence on what we reap in the future*—meaning, every choice we make today will either bring us closer or push us farther from our unique destiny. Everything we do in our current season of life will either prepare us for or propel us from that season of ultimate contribution.

Here's the good news. No matter who you are and what you've experienced up to this point in your life, you have *three tools* that can boost you toward your unique destiny:

- natural abilities
- spiritual gifts
- acquired skills

As we'll see in the remainder of this chapter, by aligning these three tools, you can reach the sweet spot I call your *unique destiny*.

Natural Abilities

Every person on this planet was born with a unique series of unteachable aptitudes, which we typically refer to as *natural abilities* or talents. I'm talking about the ability to sing in an extended vocal range. Or the ability to run a certain speed or jump a specific distance. Or the ability to process complex mathematical equations. Or the ability to create artistic expressions that are visually pleasing. Or the ability to lead others in a way that makes them eager to follow. Or high levels of hand-eye coordination. And so on and so forth.

I'm not saying these natural abilities don't need to be developed—they do. We all need to hone and mature our talents through practice and preparation. Expertise must be earned.

I am saying that specific people have a capacity for specific talents and abilities that is greater than the majority of the population. If you have a natural talent for throwing a ball at a high velocity, for example, you will have the opportunity to be a better baseball pitcher than those who lack that natural talent. You'll still need to practice. You'll still need to develop that ability. But you'll start out ahead of the curve.

I realize this isn't a popular sentiment in today's culture. Certain areas of our population deeply resent the notion that some people inherently carry a greater capacity than others for this ability or that talent. But you and I need to live in reality if we want to be true to our unique identity. And reality is that all of us fit on that bell curve. There are a few instances where we excel, and there are many instances where we lack natural ability.

Here's the important thing to remember about your talents. They are part of your unique design, which means they were planned. They were included in your DNA—your personal blueprints—for a reason.

What's more, our natural abilities play a large role in our unique discontent. Oftentimes the reason we feel so frustrated or aggravated by certain problems is that we can naturally see a better way to solve them. Once again, the problems that bother us most are likely the problems we were created to solve.

In addition, our natural abilities have a strong connection to our unique dreams. Everyone likes to excel, and the opportunity to operate out of our natural talents gives us that chance—especially when those talents have been allowed to mature and grow. In fact, our natural abilities serve as a foundation for our unique dreams by helping us identify our calling, succeed at specific roles, and work through expressions of those roles in ways that are unique to us.

Spiritual Gifts

In addition to natural abilities, those of us who have a personal relationship with God have also received *spiritual gifts* that we can use to make our difference in the world. This term gets thrown around a lot in the church, so let me offer a specific definition: *special abilities God gives every believer that he wants them to use to contribute to human flourishing.*

The Bible has a lot to say about spiritual gifts, but let me highlight one of the key passages:

There are different kinds of gifts, but the same Spirit distributes them. There are different kinds of service, but the same Lord. There are different kinds of working, but in all of them and in everyone it is the same God at work.

Now to each one the manifestation of the Spirit is given for the common good. To one there is given through the Spirit a message of wisdom, to another a message of knowledge by means of the same Spirit, to another faith by the same Spirit, to another gifts of healing by that one Spirit, to another miraculous powers, to another prophecy, to another distinguishing between spirits, to another speaking in different kinds of tongues, and to still another the interpretation of tongues. All these are the work of one and the same Spirit, and he distributes them to each one, just as he determines. (1 Corinthians 12:4–11)

Notice a number of gifts are mentioned in this passage—wisdom, knowledge, healing, faith, and so on. And certainly several other gifts are listed in other passages of Scripture. But the emphasis throughout Scripture is more on the *Giver* than on the gifts themselves. "There are different kinds of gifts, but the same Spirit distributes them."

That's important because it reminds us that the gifts we carry are *given* to us. We don't discover them or pick them up like flowers by the roadside. No, our Creator actively and intentionally gives us spiritual gifts so we can use those gifts to benefit both ourselves and others.

In the words of the apostle Peter, "Each of you should use whatever gift you have received to serve others, as faithful stewards of God's grace in its various forms" (1 Peter 4:10).

That's another important distinction. People often wonder about the difference between natural abilities and spiritual gifts. What separates one from the other? The answer is that natural talents can be used for just about any purpose, including those that are selfish or self-centered; spiritual gifts are given in order to be used to benefit the community—typically through the guidance and influence of the church.

Here's an example. Think of someone who has a natural talent for singing. Someone who can pack out a stadium and create a spectacle for an audience over the course of several hours. A true superstar. But if you were to take that same person and ask them to lead worship at your local church—meaning, sing the same songs in the same order as the regular worship leader—what would happen? More than likely, you wouldn't have the same kind of worshipful experience you're used to. Because leading others in the worship and praise of God is a different activity, a different gift, than performing.

Spiritual gifts are given in order to be used to benefit the community.

Teaching is another example. I know many gifted teachers who have the ability to take complex ideas in history or mathematics or literature or even golf and then break down the complexities and communicate them in simple ways. A lot of people have the natural ability to teach information in a way that helps others understand.

But teaching the Bible is different. It takes a special gift to start with a series of ancient texts written by about forty different authors in a completely different part of the world over a period of fifteen hundred years and then help people see how those texts both speak to and improve their lives today. That is a gift I often refer to as *uncommon sense*.

So there is a big difference between natural abilities and spiritual gifts. It's real, and it makes an impact.

Acquired Skills

The third tool we have at our disposal as we move toward our unique destiny is what I call *acquired skills*—the proficiencies or character traits we choose to develop over the course of our lives. In my experience, we typically acquire skills through one of two ways: opportunity or adversity.

For example, say you make a mean fried chicken. You know all the right ingredients and best spices to use. You've got some tricks up your sleeve that others haven't yet figured out, and you've been frying chicken for so long it's second nature. People can't get enough of it. You're known throughout your community and beyond as a fried-chicken connoisseur.

As a result of your prowess, an investor offers to help you establish a restaurant. That would be an opportunity. It's a positive moment that will force you to make some big changes and acquire new skills.

Why? Because you won't just be frying chicken anymore. You'll have to learn how to run a business. You'll be crunching numbers in addition to breadcrumbs. You'll have to figure out how to hire the right service staff and the best company for the maintenance of the building. You'll need to suss out suppliers for the best ingredients on a large scale. And so on.

These are all examples of acquired skills. You're not just learning new things because of this new opportunity; you're increasing your capacity for impact.

We also tend to acquire new skills in the middle of adversity. Let's say you lose your job, or maybe inflation is on the rise in your country and you can no longer afford to feed your family on your current salary. What do you do? You find a way to make yourself more attractive as an employee and earn a new job. Or you develop the skills necessary for a side hustle and create your own business.

This practice of acquiring skills is one of the reasons most people take a long time to reach their unique destiny. We're not typically born with those skills, but we need them to make our ultimate contribution. So as we bounce between opportunity and adversity throughout the course of our lives, we gradually become better equipped to make our ultimate contribution when the time is right.

PUT IT ALL TOGETHER

Maybe right now you're wondering, *Why am I reading about natural abilities, spiritual gifts, and acquired skills? What does this have to do with my unique destiny?*

The answer is that we are able to reach for and achieve our unique destiny only when we are ready to make our ultimate contribution to human flourishing. And what makes us ready is reaching the point in our journey where our natural abilities, spiritual gifts, and acquired skills start to click—when they intersect in a way that amplifies our impact.

That intersection is your sweet spot. It's the moment when you're able to put it all together and fully unleash the power of your unique identity.

But again, there's a process to all this. It takes both time and intention. For most of us, it takes years to understand ourselves in such a way that we start zeroing in on our natural abilities and our spiritual gifts. Some of those talents present themselves early on, but even so, we have to learn how these talents and gifts can be used in a way that contributes to human flourishing not just for ourselves but also for others.

Then it takes even more time to develop these natural abilities and gifts. To hone them. To mature. Just think back to the person you were ten years ago. Or twenty years ago. What are some of the biggest ways you've changed in that time span? What are some of the most significant ways you've grown?

When it comes to acquired skills, we rarely know what types of skill sets or character traits we will need when it comes time to make our ultimate contribution. That's why the process of life is valuable. The ups and downs. The opportunities and adversities. They polish us, refine us, and improve us until we're ready to contribute in a way that blesses not only ourselves but others.

What about you? Where are you in your journey toward your unique destiny? Your ultimate contribution?

You have a collection of natural abilities, spiritual gifts, and acquired skills. You've been carrying them and developing them for years. Maybe decades. Are you moving toward a season when you can make *your* difference in a big way?

If the answer is no, that's okay. You can turn things around as you continue coming to understand the power of your unique identity.

That's what this first section has primarily focused on—*understanding.* I've been working to lay out the concepts that I've found to be profoundly impactful in both my life and the lives of those I have coached and ministered to for twenty years and more—the concepts of *unique design, unique discontent, unique dreams,* and *unique destiny.* The reality that your difference is your superpower.

We'll keep working through these concepts in the next section—with opportunities for reviewing and for learning new things. But I'm going to shift the focus from understanding and instead help you work through the process of *embracing* these concepts. I'm going to help you not just understand them but accept them. I'm going to show you how to make them real so you can truly alter the trajectory of your life.

Finally, we're going to end the book with *unleashing* these concepts in your community and beyond. Because that is the ultimate goal: that you would not just *accept* your purpose on an intellectual or emotional level, but that you would *enact* that purpose in a way that changes lives.

Starting with your own.

PART 2

EMBRACE

CHAPTER 5

EMBRACE WHO YOU ARE

I woke up out of a dead sleep, and instantly I knew something was wrong. Really wrong.

Physically, I was experiencing something I had never encountered before. My heart was racing and palpitating wildly. *Boom boom boom!* My hands were shaking. I felt sweat beading up on my forehead and down my back.

But the most terrifying thing was what was happening in my mind. Even as I experienced those physical symptoms, I could not put together a coherent thought. I couldn't think! Everything was pure instinct. Pure reaction. Just feelings of confusion and fear and panic washing over me over and over again.

"Babe? What's going on?"

My shaking and the guttural noises coming from my throat had awakened my wife, Shameka, and she was calling out to me. She put her hand on my head, trying to get me to look at her. To focus and explain.

I couldn't. It sounds crazy to try to write about that moment all these years later, but even as I heard the words she was saying, I didn't have the ability to understand or respond. It's like my ability to reason or to rationalize anything had been suspended.

"Shun!" (That's her pet name for me.) "What's wrong?" Shameka was freaking out now, and I still couldn't do anything. I was all sensation and no control.

Finally, after a few minutes—although it felt a lot longer to me—my physical distress began to subside. My heart slowed down. The tremors ceased. I started to breathe more normally.

Then my mind returned. Have you heard people say their brain "slipped back into gear" or their thoughts "snapped back to reality"? That's what it was like. It's almost as if I could sense my consciousness getting closer and closer until my mind came back to me. My speech came back as well.

Whatever had happened to me, it was over.

That was not a fun conversation with my wife. I told her what was going on—what I had experienced. She told me I needed to see someone and get this figured out. No argument from me! I was terrified.

Thankfully, Shameka had a friend who was a counselor. We went together to have a conversation with her that same day. When I explained what had happened, the counselor said, "Dharius, it sounds like you just had an anxiety attack."

My first reaction was to shake my head, because that didn't seem right. I had never struggled with anxiety before. I've never been a fearful person. I didn't have any family history of anxiety or depression or those types of things. I was in my early thirties and physically healthy. I was taking good care of myself. How could I have an anxiety attack?

The counselor said, "Dharius, sometimes things like this are chemical. But sometimes they are situational. So what's going on in your life right now?"

"Oh." Shameka glanced over at me with one of those looks wives often give. I rubbed the back of my head kind of sheepishly. There was a lot going on in my life in that particular season. Too much.

For starters, I was in the final semester of my doctoral program at Fuller Theological Seminary. The deadline for my dissertation was soon approaching. On top of that, I was in the middle of writing my first book—speeding toward another big deadline. What's more, our church had been experiencing exponential growth, which meant I was trying to lead two building campaigns at the same time—one of which included a contentious legal fight that had been dragging on for two interminable years because certain people were unhappy about seeing a church invade their community. On top of that, I was preaching every Sunday, leading a weekly Bible study, officiating weddings and funerals in our congregation, plus showing up for all the extra programs and events pastors typically attend. Oh, and in addition to all that, I was doing my best to be an attentive husband and an engaged father to my two sons.

So, yes, there was a lot going on. So much that my brain and body were threatening to rebel. To shut down.

Thankfully, God is sovereign, and he was about to give me a real-time lesson in his providence.

My anxiety attack happened in the middle of the week. That Sunday afternoon, I flew out to Fuller for the final class of my doctoral program. The professor for that class was Dr. Archibald Hart, who had formerly been the dean of Fuller's School of Psychology. The subject of the class was "The Minister's Personal Health." Hello! Dr. Hart spent an entire week working through subjects like self-image issues, approval addiction, the coopting of pastoral ministry by culture, and more. He also gave the podium to his daughter, a therapist and life coach, who spoke about dealing with internal issues and managing life the right way.

It was exactly what I needed to hear. All of it. I came out of that week with two big conclusions: I needed to see a therapist, and I needed a life coach. I was serious too. I didn't just think about it; I made the appointments and got to work.

In the months and years that followed, I came to understand that the source of my anxiety wasn't being overworked or feeling burned-out or trying to accomplish too much. All of those were true in my life, but each one was just another symptom.

The root issue causing me to struggle was that I had failed to accept my uniqueness. I had failed to embrace my unique identity.

EMBRACING YOUR UNIQUENESS

Here's a principle I have found to be true both personally and in the lives of those I have coached and counseled over the years: *God will not honor the direction of our lives when we are living outside of our unique identity.*

God will not honor the direction of our lives when we are living outside of our unique identity.

I'm not saying God will abandon you. I'm not saying God will reject you or curse you when you choose a life that is disconnected from your unique identity.

I am saying God will not honor that. Why? Because God created and crafted you intentionally, for a unique reason and purpose. He knows exactly who he designed you to be and exactly what he designed you to do and achieve. He built you with a purpose in mind—with a specific plan for you to contribute not just to overall human flourishing but to your own flourishing. We are actively dishonoring God when we reject that plan and choose to walk away from our unique identity; therefore, it should come as no surprise when God refuses to honor that choice.

In other words, God won't help you become someone God has not created you to be.

That's what I discovered after my anxiety attack. See, ever since accepting my calling to be a pastor, I had attempted to follow the example of several church leaders I admired. My father was at the top of that list, but there were several other pastors whose personality traits and leadership styles I sought to emulate.

> **God won't help you become someone God has not created you to be.**

That is a natural impulse for all passions and professions. As we try to get our feet under us in the pursuit of our calling, we instinctively look around at others who are succeeding in that calling and seek to emulate what they are doing well.

The problem comes when emulating others pulls us away from who we are at our core—when it causes us to drift out of our unique identity. That's what I experienced.

To give you some examples, I know a lot of pastors out there who largely follow a "chaplain method" approach to ministry. Such pastors make it a point to be present within their community and alongside their congregations whenever possible. Sunday morning. Sunday evening. Wednesday evening. Counseling. Hospital visitation. Prison ministry. Budget meetings. If anything is happening or *could* happen at the church, those pastors are present for the occasion.

I tried to emulate those pastors by adopting a similar

approach. For much of my early ministry, I was the one opening and closing the church doors whenever something was going on.

Also, many of the pastors and leaders I admired were authors with high-profile platforms. They wrote books. They traveled extensively to speak at conferences and guest lecture at other congregations. They were constantly out there preaching, teaching, and presenting the Word in every season.

So whenever I got a chance to speak, I took it. I assumed it was my responsibility. And when a publisher approached me with a book contract, I jumped at the chance.

Another trend that was popular among several pastors I admired—largely my peers in terms of age—was multisite ministry. The idea for many in my generation was that technology meant we were no longer limited to a specific geographical location. We could expand our work and our ministry to several campuses through the magic of video, which is why I found myself managing two building projects for two new campuses at the same time. People were responding in those communities. There was a great opportunity for effective ministry, and I felt responsible to come through.

To be clear, there is nothing wrong with any of those approaches to ministry. The multisite approach has been effective in many places and many congregations (including my own). Pastors and leaders have blessed many readers through the self-giving act of publishing. And I have personally witnessed the power of faithful shepherds whose physical presence is welcome and necessary within their flock.

Yet my attempts to achieve a combination of all those approaches—and to do so all at the same time—was the wrong choice for me. Why? Because it pulled me away from my unique identity. I was trying to approach pastoral ministry through the experiences of others rather than living out my own calling as myself.

The same can be true of you. In fact, if you are experiencing struggle and strife in your attempts to live out your calling or achieve a sense of meaning and purpose, there's a good chance you are living outside of your unique identity. Which means there's a good chance God will not honor your effort.

That's the bad news. The good news is you can get back on the right track by embracing your unique identity.

We have already discussed the basic elements of your unique identity: your unique design, your unique discontent, your unique dreams, and your unique destiny. Such understanding is crucial because until you understand something needs to be done, you have no hope of doing it.

But there is a big difference between understanding the concept of unique identity on an intellectual level and actually *accepting* that truth for your life. To say it another way, it's one thing to understand and believe that all people are unique; it's another thing entirely to embrace *your own* uniqueness.

You have a unique identity—and your identity is *valuable*. Your difference is your destiny. *You* as an individual are unlike any other individual on this planet, and that *is* good news.

FROM JACOB TO ISRAEL

I've shared a lot about myself in this chapter, which is intentional. I want you to know that I have been down the road I am encouraging you to walk. But this is a good time to take a look at someone else's story. Specifically, I want to show you how the life of the Old Testament patriarch Jacob is a helpful illustration of what it means to not only *understand* the concept of uniqueness but to *embrace* your own unique identity.

Let's start with the beginning of that story:

> Isaac prayed to the LORD on behalf of his wife, because she was childless. The LORD answered his prayer, and his wife Rebekah became pregnant. The babies jostled each other within her, and she said, "Why is this happening to me?" So she went to inquire of the LORD.
>
> The LORD said to her,
>
> > "Two nations are in your womb,
> >   and two peoples from within you will be separated;
> > one people will be stronger than the other,
> >   and the older will serve the younger."
>
> When the time came for her to give birth, there were twin boys in her womb. The first to come out was red, and his whole body was like a hairy garment; so they named him Esau. After this, his brother came out, with his hand grasping Esau's heel; so he was named Jacob. Isaac was sixty years old when Rebekah gave birth to them. (Genesis 25:21–26)

I want to point out two things about Jacob from these verses. The first is that God revealed key components of Jacob's unique identity even before he was born. God said to Rebekah, "Two nations are in your womb." Which means that Jacob came into this world preprogrammed with a legacy. He wasn't simply going to be successful as an individual; he was going to be the forefather of an entire nation. Even more, Jacob's line of descendants would be stronger and more influential than that of his older brother Esau. That's significant, because in the culture of the ancient world, it was the firstborn son who typically carried and expanded a family's legacy.

Here's the second thing I want you to notice about Jacob. In addition to receiving a window into his unique destiny at birth, he was also given a destructive label. The name Jacob means "he grasps the heel," which in the ancient world was an idiom for deception. Basically, Jacob was named "Deceiver" because of the circumstances of his birth.

Talk about a tough label to live down!

Not surprisingly, Jacob did not live that label down. Instead, he wrapped it around his heart. We know this to be true because of all the famous Bible stories that involve Jacob's deceptive actions. He tricked his brother, Esau, out of his birthright for a bowl of stew. He conned his father, Isaac, into blessing the younger son instead of the older. Jacob even got into an extended battle of deception with his father-in-law, Laban, during more than twenty years of living and working together under the same roof.

For much of his early life, Jacob was a schemer. He was a conniver. He was a selfish grifter. Those are the labels he wore on his chest, and those were the vehicles through which he presented himself to the world.

Just one problem. Those labels did not match his unique identity. Those descriptions did not jibe with who God had created Jacob to be and all that God intended Jacob to achieve. Therefore, God confronted Jacob by means of a heavenly wrestling match in order to get him back on the right track:

> So Jacob was left alone, and a man wrestled with him till daybreak. When the man saw that he could not overpower him, he touched the socket of Jacob's hip so that his hip was

wrenched as he wrestled with the man. Then the man said, "Let me go, for it is daybreak."

But Jacob replied, "I will not let you go unless you bless me."

The man asked him, "What is your name?"

"Jacob," he answered.

Then the man said, "Your name will no longer be Jacob, but Israel, because you have struggled with God and with humans and have overcome." (Genesis 32:24–28)

There is so much to unpack in this passage because this was a critical moment—not just in Jacob's life but in all of biblical history. There's a lot going on. But I want to highlight two specific moments that have direct application to this idea of unique identity.

The first is when God reminded Jacob of his unique identity by overwriting his old label with a new and better name. Remember, Jacob means, figuratively, "he who deceives." In this passage, God gave him a new name, Israel, which means "he struggles with God." I know to some people that may not sound like much of an improvement, but think about it. You don't struggle with someone you don't care about. You don't engage with someone you don't care for.

God removed Jacob's false identity—the schemer. The conniver. The grifter. God said, in effect, "Put away those old labels because they don't reflect who you really are. And who you really are is a person who will grapple with me because you are known by me. More than that, who you really are is the founder of a nation who will grapple with me because they will be my people."

Notice that God didn't give Jacob a new identity. Jacob's legacy as the founder of a nation had been set in stone even before his birth. Instead, God reminded Jacob of who he really was. He reminded Jacob of his unique identity.

Now let's look at the second moment, which I love. This is the moment when Jacob began to embrace his unique identity, and it came when he cried out, "I will not let you go unless you bless me." I love that!

This man who had been labeled as a schemer, a cheater, and a liar had the audacity to grab hold of God and refuse to let go. He clung to God and said, "I will not let you go unless you bless me." Why is that important? Because it reveals the moment when Jacob finally saw himself as a person of worth— the moment he finally saw himself as a person who didn't have to steal what was valuable but could receive it as a gift.

That was the moment Jacob finally realized he was worthy to be blessed. He embraced that truth even as he received his new name.

When I say you need to *embrace* your unique identity, I don't simply mean you should *accept* who you are. Because that's easy. All of us can accept things we don't like. Jim got the promotion I felt like I deserved, but I'm going to accept it and keep working hard. I'm not being treated right in this relationship, but I can accept that my spouse isn't perfect. The doctor called with bad news, but I've accepted my fate.

It's not that acceptance is a bad thing. Accepting who you are is an important step in embracing your unique identity—but it's only a first step.

> **When you receive the truth that you are a treasure, you have begun to embrace your unique identity.**

The real work comes when you *value* who you are. When you realize that you have significance simply because you are the handiwork of a Master Craftsman. When you receive the truth that you are a treasure, you have begun to embrace your unique identity.

IDENTIFY YOURSELF

I've seen a lot of cops-and-robbers–type movies come and go throughout my lifetime. There's always a scene in those movies when a law enforcement agent is running around trying to track down the bad guy, and they come across someone unexpected.

What do the cop types always say in those moments?

"Identify yourself!"

That's what I want you to do. I want you to identify yourself so you can begin the crucial work of embracing your unique identity. Specifically, I want you to identify the four elements of your unique identity that we explored in the first four chapters: design, discontent, dreams, and destiny.

Why go through this exercise? Because you can't embrace something you don't recognize. You can't value something if you haven't identified what makes it valuable.

Including yourself.

Your Unique Design

What are the key characteristics of your unique design? We explored that concept in the first chapter, and I've mentioned it several times in several ways throughout these pages. If you've come this far, I know you understand the concept.

But how does that concept apply to *you*? How is it fleshed out in *your* life right now—today? What is *your* unique design?

Here are some questions to help you zero in on what makes you unique:

- Who are you? What are some key ingredients that make up your personality?
- What can you achieve or accomplish at a higher level than most other people? What do you do well?
- What are the main experiences that have shaped your life so far?

Now it's time to pick up a pen or pencil and write about your unique identity. Use the space below to write down what it is that makes you *you*. And yes, I'm serious about this. Remember, you can't embrace what you haven't identified.

So go ahead and identify who you are.

_____

_____

_____

_____

_____

_____

This next part is important. In fact, it's critical. What you've done so far is identify your unique design. You have taken the intellectual step of thinking about who you are and writing it down. That's good. It's helpful.

But now it's time to begin the process of *embracing* that design. Those things you wrote down are true about you, which makes them valuable because you are valuable. Those things you wrote down didn't come from you; they came from your Creator. They were intentionally programmed into you by your Creator.

Wrap your mind around this truth—that your differences are not deficiencies. No! Your differences are your superpower. Because you have a unique design.

Your Unique Discontent

Let's go through the same process with your unique discontent. Remember, the problems that bother you most are very likely the problems you were created to solve.

So what bothers you? What irritates and agitates you? Again, use these questions to think through your unique discontent:

- What are some specific incidents that have made you feel notably upset in recent months—so upset that you haven't stopped thinking about them?
- What are some injustices, inequities, or inequalities that make you feel angry? Where do you bristle because something isn't fair?
- What kind of needs grab your attention most? Meaning, what is it that people need that you wish you could provide?
- What are issues or circumstances that seem to bother you way more than they bother others?

What are the elements that make up your unique discontent? How would you describe it? It's time to buckle down. Use the space below to write what you believe is true.

Your Unique Dreams

Next, what are your unique dreams? Remember, these are not specific goals or target achievements as much as the activities and circumstances that catch your attention in a big way. We're talking about the things you do that cause your eyes to sparkle and your mind to wake up.

As we learned in chapter 3, *the opportunities that inspire you most are often the opportunities you were created to seize.*

What does that look like for you? Here are some questions to help you think it through:

- What parts of your daily work make you feel energized?
- What do you feel passionate about?
- Which of your accomplishments make you feel most proud and most satisfied?
- What are the opportunities that make you feel most inspired and most alive?

Time to write again. Use the space below to summarize or describe your unique dreams to the best of your ability.

Your Unique Destiny

This is the final of your four *D*s, and I understand it's a little more difficult to identify—because you probably haven't experienced it yet. That's okay.

As a reminder, your unique destiny is your ultimate contribution to human flourishing. It's not your only contribution, nor is it the only contribution that matters. But it is your magnum opus. It's the season when your natural abilities, spiritual gifts, and acquired skills line up in just the right way and allow you to make a huge impact in the world.

If you have already lived through such a season, by all means go ahead and write down your unique destiny in the space below. If you are still wondering what your ultimate contribution might be, use these questions to spur your thinking:

- What do you want to be remembered for by future generations?
- If you could accomplish one big thing in your lifetime, what would you like it to be?
- What do you want to be your ultimate contribution to human flourishing?

Pencil time again. Write down your best thoughts and hopes when it comes to your unique destiny.

TIME FOR A HUG

Some counselors and psychologists employ a technique called "self-hugging." It's not a complicated technique. In fact, it's exactly what it sounds like—patients are encouraged to wrap their arms around their own bodies and give themselves a hug.

So, not complicated—but in many cases, surprisingly effective.

According to research, the practice of self-hugging has been known to reduce physical pain in patients. It can help people feel safer in a world that gets more and more chaotic every day. It often improves a patient's mood and can help individuals feel more positive about themselves—happier in their own skin.[1]

The idea of embracing your unique identity is similar to the practice of self-hugging. I'm asking you to mentally and emotionally wrap your arms around yourself and embrace who you are. Not who you *wish* you were or who you *think* you should be—but *who you are.*

Yes, there is room for improvement. Yes, you have faults and flaws that could use some maturation. So does everyone else. That's okay.

The things you wrote down about yourself in the last few pages of this book are a representation of your unique identity. They are just words on a page, I know, but they are words about *you.* So embrace them. Talk to yourself about them. Encourage yourself with them.

Choose to value who you are, just as your Creator values who you are.

If you can't do that—if you feel unsatisfied or unimpressed by what you've written down in these pages—then there may well be some obstacles in your life that are preventing you from embracing your unique identity. Those obstacles need to be addressed, and we'll do just that in the next chapter.

CHAPTER 6

EVALUATE HOW YOU GOT HERE

A s a man thinks in his heart, so is he."

The person who originally wrote that statement is famous. You've heard of him, I'm sure. He was a leader. He was an entrepreneur. He was a teacher. He was a poet. He was fantastically wealthy. Because of those factors and more, he was one of the most celebrated individuals throughout the entire world during his lifetime.

His name was Solomon, and even today he is recognized as one of the wisest individuals to have walked this planet.

But consider that statement for a minute. Chew on it. Why would Solomon say, "As a man thinks in his heart, so is he" (Proverbs 23:7, my translation)? After all, Solomon was steeped in the hierarchical system of Israel's kingdom. He was born the son of a king, which made him royalty. He mingled with powerful people in society—the advisers and officials and head stewards. He gave orders to servants and soldiers. He watched the priests and teachers of the law. He passed by the peasants and commoners whenever he walked the streets.

Shouldn't Solomon have said, "As a man is born to his class, so is he"?

What about education? Solomon received the finest training available to a young man of his day. He learned from the best teachers and tutors. He had access to the biggest library. He was offered the most interesting apprenticeships and hands-on learning opportunities. Shouldn't Solomon have said, "As a man educates his mind, so is he"?

Then there's money. When I say Solomon was fantastically wealthy, I don't mean the kind of "wealthy" we typically think of in today's world—stock options and portfolios and all that. Nope. The people of my generation might understand it best when I say Solomon was Scrooge-McDuck rich. Remember the TV show *DuckTales*? Scrooge had a huge vault filled with gold and jewels and other precious items, and he would literally dive in and splash around through all that wealth like it was a swimming pool.

That was Solomon. From his earliest memories, his life was bathed in money and resources. So shouldn't he have written, "As a man fills his bank account, so is he"?

Solomon didn't say any of that. Instead, he declared that you and I will become *what we think*. He laid down the powerful principle that who we are and how we live is tethered to how we think.

Who we are and how we live is tethered to how we think.

This is a profound perception when we apply it to the primary theme we've been exploring throughout these pages. Check this out. You have a unique identity that was programmed into your life by your Creator long before you were even conceived. At the same time, your life is profoundly influenced by your thoughts. "As a man thinks, so is he."

When you put these two ideas together, here's what they

produce: *God wants you to think about you the way he thinks about you so you can act like the you he created you to be rather than the you you've always been.*

Whew! That's a mouthful, I know, but it's a crucial concept. God wants you to think about yourself the way he thinks about you. Which means he wants you to think about yourself in terms of your unique identity—in terms of who he created you to be. Why? So that you can live an abundant life. So that you can act like *the you* he created, *the you* he intended, instead of the counterfeit you that has been walking around in your shoes for years. Or decades.

In other words, when you think of yourself the way God thinks of you, you will inevitably begin to live the life God wants for you. That's the principle.

HOW DID YOU GET HERE?

That principle is simple enough, right? When you and I think of ourselves the way God thinks of us, we will operate out of our unique identity and live the kind of life God wants for us. The kind of life God planned for us and designed us to carry out.

But that raises an important question: Why is it so hard to follow that principle? Why is it so hard for me to see myself the way God sees me? Why is it so hard for most people to understand and embrace their unique identity? Why is it so hard for most of us to do the things we were created to do?

Think about it. When someone does a good job building a tool, that tool does a good job fulfilling its purpose. A screwdriver doesn't need much help driving in screws or pulling them back out. When installed correctly, a garage door opener doesn't need a bunch of extra attention or concentration in order to open and close it. Things that are designed strategically carry out that design automatically.

Why are you any different? Think of all the mental energy you've spent trying to identify your purpose. Trying to find meaning. Think of all the time you've wasted trying to assert yourself in careers, callings, or missions you were never meant to undertake. Think of all the false starts you've had to endure because you were trying to live up to other people's expectations rather than embracing your uniqueness.

It's not just you. It's all of us. So many people in this world are flailing around in their attempts to both identify their purpose and carry it out. But why?

Why is it so hard?

It's not that you were designed incorrectly. Not even close. The God who ignited the sun and set the planets of our solar system in their proper orbits is the same Creator who programmed your DNA. You were crafted with intention. You were planned *with* purpose *for* a purpose. There is nothing random or accidental about who you are.

It's not that you're too complicated either. The food chain is complicated. Photosynthesis is complicated. The strong force that holds atoms together both in your body and throughout the entire universe is complicated. But all of these systems operate as their Designer intended.

In my experience, the reason we so often fail to understand and embrace our unique wiring is that there are obstacles that hinder or even fully block us from doing so. Some of these obstacles are confined to the present moment, but most of them have deep roots in the past.

We're going to explore four categories of these obstacles: emotional, relational, cultural, and spiritual. But these obstacles are multifaceted. They are layered with complexity. We'll discuss each category separately because we are dealing with words that need to make sense. But it's important to understand that these obstacles are not separated in the context of our lives. In the real world, they're woven together. They pile on top of each other. And they combine in painful ways to drag us down when we should be sprinting forward in the strength of our unique identity.

EMOTIONAL OBSTACLES

The first type of obstacle that prevents people from embracing their unique identity is what I call *emotional obstacles*. These are obstacles connected to the way we see ourselves—to what we believe about ourselves. That's crucial because, as we just saw, "As a man thinks, so is he."

Importantly, emotional obstacles are internal. They might not originate with you—in fact, most of the emotional obstacles we face are caused by other people—but they do reside within your own heart and mind. You carry them internally.

In this way, emotional obstacles have the propensity to sabotage your ability to live out of your unique identity and strive toward your unique destiny. All of this is an inside job.

I've found that stories are often a great way to explain and illustrate complex ideas, so I'm going to work through the idea of emotional obstacles in the context of Moses's story from the Bible. If that surprises you, I understand. Most of us think of Moses as a pillar of biblical history, and rightly so. Moses was the miracle man. The one who confronted Pharaoh with a cry of, "Let my people go!" The one who liberated God's people from slavery. The one who called down the ten plagues.

The one who watched with his staff raised as God divided the Red Sea. The one who met with God "face to face, as one speaks to a friend" (Exodus 33:11).

It's true that Moses eventually embraced his unique identity and achieved his unique destiny. But it took some doing. It took some learning. And it certainly required Moses to overcome several emotional obstacles along the way.

Think back to Moses's origin. He was supposed to be killed as a baby, remember? Pharaoh ordered that all male children among the Hebrews be thrown into the Nile River, but Moses's mother—a woman bursting with cleverness and courage—defied that order by placing her baby in a "papyrus basket" coated with pitch. She also had Miriam, Moses's sister, watch the baby to see what happened. Here's what Miriam saw: Pharaoh's daughter found the basket, retrieved Moses, and determined to adopt him as her own son.

Here's a detail many people miss when they hear Moses's story:

> Then his sister asked Pharaoh's daughter, "Shall I go and get one of the Hebrew women to nurse the baby for you?"
>
> "Yes, go," she answered. So the girl went and got the baby's mother. Pharaoh's daughter said to her, "Take this baby and nurse him for me, and I will *pay you*." So the woman took the baby and nursed him. When the child grew older, she took him to Pharaoh's daughter and he became her son. She named him Moses, saying, "I drew him out of the water." (Exodus 2:7–10, emphasis added)

First of all, Miriam obviously took after her mother, because that was some quick thinking. But the end result of all these events is that Moses's mother got paid to raise her own child. Then after several years, Moses was transferred to the household of Pharaoh.

So he was supposed to be killed. Then he was rescued. Then he had a brief period living with his parents in a typical Hebrew home. Then he became royalty. Later, he witnessed one of the Egyptian guards beating a Hebrew slave—one of Moses's own people. In a fit of rage, Moses killed the guard. He became a murderer. And when Pharaoh caught wind of what had happened, he tried to kill his own adopted grandson. Which meant Moses became an exile. He fled from Egypt and settled in Midian, where he started a family and tended sheep for forty years.[1]

Self-Esteem Issues

Do you see the potential for emotional obstacles in Moses's life? The potential for issues connected to how he saw himself? After decades of living, Moses thought he was a screwup! A failure. A man who had missed the boat for whatever calling he was supposed to achieve.

Then God showed up through a burning bush. He told Moses, "So now, go. I am sending you to Pharaoh to bring my people the Israelites out of Egypt" (Exodus 3:10).

Talk about calling! Talk about purpose! God himself shows up and tells Moses exactly what he wants him to do: set an entire nation free from slavery. That was Moses's unique destiny. His ultimate contribution to human flourishing, right there on a silver platter.

How did Moses respond? He griped. He groused. He wheedled and whined. He told God all the reasons he wasn't the right man for the job, and he ultimately said, "O my Lord, please send by the hand of whomever else You may send" (4:13 NKJV). In other words, "Find someone else."

In that moment, Moses was confronted by an emotional obstacle. Specifically, he was blocked from embracing his unique identity because of esteem issues.

See, God told Moses he had been designed and handcrafted to deliver the Israelites from slavery. But Moses couldn't get past his failures from the past. Moses couldn't picture himself as a leader. He couldn't conceive of himself as a deliverer. He couldn't reconcile the vision of what God was calling him to do with the self-generated reality that Moses was a failure fit for nothing more important than tending sheep.

I see people engaged in a similar struggle with esteem issues today. Regularly. I'm always surprised when I talk with someone who is obviously talented and equipped with the gifts and skills needed to make a huge impact in their chosen fields—but they can't see it. They don't value themselves, nor do they appreciate everything they have to offer.

In short, because they don't see themselves as God sees them, they are blocked from embracing their unique identity.

People-Pleasing Tendencies

Another emotional obstacle that often hinders folks from embracing their unique identity is what I call *people-pleasing tendencies*. Which means basing our value and self-worth not on what God thinks about us or even what we think of ourselves but on what other people think of us.

All of us experience that tendency to some degree. When you've worked really hard to create something special in your house, you get that flush of excitement when your spouse comes home. You hover around as they walk through the door, waiting for them to notice. Waiting for them to see and be pleased. Or when you pour yourself into a project at work, you don't just turn it in and move on. You wait for some kind of acknowledgment. Some kind of evaluation. Some kind of approval.

That's normal and natural—in short bursts. But it becomes unnatural when pleasing other people is the primary mission of our lives. It becomes harmful when pleasing others is the basis on which we evaluate our own worth.

Again, Moses's story offers an effective illustration of this principle:

> The next day Moses took his seat to serve as judge for the people, and they stood around him from morning till evening. When his father-in-law saw all that Moses was doing for the people, he said, "What is this you are doing for the people? Why do you alone sit as judge, while all these people stand around you from morning till evening?"
>
> Moses answered him, "Because the people come to me to seek God's will. Whenever they have a dispute, it is brought to me, and I decide between the parties and inform them of God's decrees and instructions." (Exodus 18:13–16)

This was after the Israelites' miraculous exodus from Egypt, while they were still wandering in the wilderness. We're talking about hundreds of thousands of people, yet Moses was the only arbitrator among them. In his mind, and apparently in the minds of the Israelites, Moses was the only one able to "seek God's will" and determine what should be done when any conflict erupted within the community. "He stole my ox," "Their children attacked my children," "His tent is too close to my tent." And on and on.

Now, you know the people of Israel were happy with this arrangement. This is like if you or I had a problem, we could just go right to the Oval Office and ask the president to hear our complaint. Straight to the top. You know if Twitter had existed during Moses's day, there would have been some very happy Israelites tweeting about Moses. "Oh, he spent ten minutes talking with me about my problem. He was so attentive!"

Here's the problem: Moses had a divine calling—he had a unique destiny—and that calling did not include living as Judge Judy every day. No, that calling was to liberate God's people and bring them to the promised land. That was Moses's ultimate contribution.

So why did he spend so much time serving as judge for the people? Part of the answer, it seems to me, is that Moses felt responsible as a leader, and he genuinely believed he was doing the right thing. He felt like he was the only one who could intercede for the Israelites. But I also think a significant part of Moses enjoyed the attention. Remember, Moses had self-esteem issues. He had previously believed himself to be a failure. Now, all of a sudden, all of these people needed him. They wanted his opinion. His advice. His leadership.

And Moses wanted to make them happy. He wanted to please his audience.

It took Jethro, Moses's father-in-law, to finally step in and say, "What you are doing is not good. You and these people who come to you will only wear yourselves out" (Exodus 18:17–18).

Again, this issue affects many people today. Some of us were created by God for a specific purpose, but we spend a huge amount of time and energy trying to please other people rather than carrying out God's purpose. Rather than live out of our unique identity, we behave the way other people want us to behave so that those people will be pleased. Or proud. Or happy.

We are chameleons. And a decision to blend in rather than accept our uniqueness becomes an obstacle that blocks us from embracing our unique identity.

Soul Wounds

I could address a lot of other emotional obstacles. I could provide tons of additional examples of how issues inside us prevent us from embracing who we are. But in my experience, most of those emotional obstacles can be summarized by what I call *soul wounds*.

The definition of a soul wound is just what it sounds like—it's a moment we receive damage or an injury, not to our physical body, but to our soul. To the person we are inside. And in the same way physical injuries will fester if they are not treated properly and allowed to heal, soul wounds can become infected when they are never resolved.

The problem is that soul wounds are much easier to ignore than physical wounds. Right? Physical injuries are right out there in the open, gushing blood or keeping someone on the couch because their back is out again. These situations demand to be addressed. Soul wounds, on the other hand, can be pushed down. Hushed up. Even forgotten.

Rejection is an example of a soul wound. Let's say your father left the house when you were young and didn't come back. You got a phone call every now and then, but no birthday cards. No Christmas get-togethers. He didn't show up at any of your games or recitals. He didn't do anything that made you feel like he cared about you or wanted to be a part of your life in any meaningful way.

That's a soul wound. It's an injury. And the statement "time heals all wounds" is a lie. If we don't deal with the pain and the harm of that rejection, it will lead to internal infection.

There are many kinds of soul wounds. Neglect. Abuse. Manipulation. Bullying. Trauma. Addiction. Failure. I'm sure others come to your mind as well. We're all familiar with the kinds of injuries that can produce soul wounds, even if we don't understand the way these injuries linger.

Once again, soul wounds that go untreated often become infected, which means they start to leak out into our regular lives through harmful symptoms. Some of those symptoms are easy to identify. When we encounter people with low self-esteem or the diseases of despair I mentioned earlier—anxiety, depression, suicide, and so on—we understand those people likely endured something traumatic in their past.

But an infected soul wound can also produce symptoms we don't expect. Arrogance and narcissism can be caused by soul wounds. A person has been rejected to the point where they no longer allow themselves to get close to another individual, because getting close risks being rejected again. So they act out. They adopt a persona to keep everyone at arm's length.

My point is this: our society often functions as if anybody who isn't regularly seeing a therapist must be emotionally stable in every way. *If I don't need pills, then nothing is going on.* But that's not the case.

All of us have experienced soul wounds, but most of us have never resolved them. As a result, the symptoms of those soul wounds often become emotional obstacles that prevent us from embracing our unique identity.

RELATIONAL OBSTACLES

The second category of obstacles that prevent people from embracing their unique identity is *relational*, which means obstacles hinder us from embracing our true selves that originate in and are maintained by our relationships—typically our closest relationships. This happens when we allow other people to dictate who we are and what we are called to do rather than living out of our unique identity.

We've talked a lot about Moses in this chapter, so let me jump over to another example. Here is the origin story of a man named Gideon:

> The angel of the LORD came and sat down under the oak in Ophrah that belonged to Joash the Abiezrite, where his son Gideon was threshing wheat in a winepress to keep it from the Midianites. When the angel of the LORD appeared to Gideon, he said, "The LORD is with you, mighty warrior."
>
> "Pardon me, my lord," Gideon replied, "but if the LORD is with us, why has all this happened to us? Where are all his wonders that our ancestors told us about when they said, 'Did not the LORD bring us up out of Egypt?' But now the LORD has abandoned us and given us into the hand of Midian."
>
> The LORD turned to him and said, "Go in the strength you have and save Israel out of Midian's hand. Am I not sending you?"
>
> "Pardon me, my lord," Gideon replied, "but how can I save Israel? My clan is the weakest in Manasseh, and I am the least in my family." (Judges 6:11–15)

First of all, do you see the soul wound in these verses? An angel of God appears to Gideon, calls him a "mighty warrior," and commissions him to "save Israel out of Midian's hand."

This was the dream, right? Children in that day knew the history of their people. They knew the heroes. Even Gideon mentioned all the "wonders that our ancestors told us about." How many Israelite boys in Gideon's day imagined they were Moses leading the Israelites out of slavery? Or Joshua leading the armies of Israel against the Canaanites? And now those dreams have come true for Gideon. The angel is right there in front of him. *Save your people.*

Yet Gideon immediately shrank back. Look at what he said: "My clan is the weakest in Manasseh, and I am the least in my family." Gideon had been told he was worthless for so long that he believed it internally. Unquestioningly. He wore a label on his chest that read, "The least." Less than. Unimportant.

Gideon had a soul wound. And when you dig into the Scriptures a little deeper, it becomes clear that Gideon's soul wound traced back to the relationships in his life. I say that because God designed Gideon to be a warrior. A liberator. A leader. But his family didn't see him that way. They saw him as too young and too weak, which is why the angel found him hiding away in a hole in the ground doing his best to thresh wheat—the job of a servant.

Relational obstacles are huge today. If I had to guess, I'd say they are likely a big factor in *your* life, whether you recognize it or not. Why? Because there are people in your life who have strong opinions about who you are, who you should become, and what you should do. Even if you're older and established in a career, some of the people you care about will feel the need to tell you who you are rather than allowing you to determine who God created you to be.

Here's the principle: *your ability to navigate these relational dynamics will go a long way toward determining the degree to which you accept and embrace your unique identity.*

CULTURAL OBSTACLES

The third category of obstacles to embracing our unique wiring is what I call *cultural.* Our exploration of these obstacles is expanding outward. Emotional obstacles are highly personal. Yes, there are soul wounds and other issues that can be caused by other people, but you and I carry them internally. They reside with us. Relational obstacles involve a wider net. The people closest to us either boost or impede our ability to embrace our unique identity. With cultural obstacles, the net is wider still.

Culture is one of those words with many different meanings to different people. For this discussion, let's define culture as *the collection of values, priorities, and beliefs that are accepted by a majority of people in a specific region or location.* To put it another way, it is the water in which you swim.

Now when it comes to things like calling, purpose, and unique identity, we must understand there are certain ways of being and doing that are more celebrated and socially acceptable in a culture than others. Some professions and personal identifiers are lifted up within a specific culture, and others are frowned on. They don't carry as much weight.

My pastor talks about this sometimes. He told me, "If I were in any other line of work, people would call me a genius. But because I'm in pastoral ministry, I'm everything but that."

He's right. This is a man who started an organization from scratch in Cleveland, Ohio. He developed hundreds of thousands of square feet of property. He employs a hundred people on his staff. His organization invests millions of dollars into his community every year. Yet people still see him as "just a preacher."

Let's be honest about the state of things. If you live in the United States or another Western nation, then you live in a culture that places a high esteem on earning a lot of money. On having influence. On garnering power. You also live in a culture that in many ways overvalues education—or more specifically, educational degrees. And you live in a culture that praises people for working too much and damaging themselves physically in order to achieve those things society values.

Therefore, if you have been designed in a way that does not align with those cultural expectations, your culture will be an obstacle that can hinder you from embracing that design. If you have a divine calling and purpose that are different from what your culture says is important, you are going to feel the tension of that difference, and you'll likely feel it every day. That's the reality.

For example, maybe God has called you to spend a season of your life raising children and pouring yourself into the next generation. Or maybe God has equipped you for the kind of honest work that keeps society running—building homes, fixing machinery, or driving trucks. Or maybe your role is to serve others through teaching, counseling, cooking, and so on.

There are many roles and callings that are not highly esteemed or respected within our society. And if your unique identity leads you into one of those roles or callings, you will need to decide which voice will carry the most weight in your decision making—God's voice or the voice of culture.

Let me say this as well. In addition to "culture" in a broad sense, there are many subcultures that influence us in many ways. Religion is a good example. If you grew up in church or are currently part of a specific denomination, you will face specific pressures related to how you see yourself and what you do. Religious groups can have cemented opinions when it comes to which work is and isn't valued, what people of different genders could or should accomplish, and so on.

Race and class are also examples. Our culture tends to pigeonhole people of different ethnicities and socioeconomic strata into specific roles. *Because you look like that, you should only try to do this.* And to be frank, there's also a sense in which many people are stereotyped within the context of their own race or class. If you start to think or behave in ways that are inconsistent with "the way we do things," you may encounter a challenge or a rebuke. *You're not really one of us.*

My point is this: *your culture and subcultures will invariably produce certain scripts that outline what is and is not appropriate for you.* That will happen. That pressure will come.

You have to decide whether you will allow that pressure to prevent you from embracing your unique identity.

SPIRITUAL OBSTACLES

The final category of obstacles that hinder us from accepting and embracing who we are is *spiritual.* It is connected to the reality that you are an eternal being created by an eternal God for an eternal purpose. The obstacle comes from an enemy who is against all that.

Have you ever watched those press conferences that coaches give after losing a game? They say some funny things. "We didn't execute our game plan as we had anticipated." Or "what you saw on the field tonight is not a representation of who we are or how we do things." A lot of words but little substance, you know what I mean?

Here's what coaches rarely say: "Our opponent is just way better at this sport than we are." You never hear that, even though most of the time it's the truth!

In the same way, you and I need to recognize that we are not playing this game called life on our own. We have an opponent. Specifically, we have a spiritual enemy who hates our Creator, hates us because we are his creations, and is bound and determined to do whatever it takes to prevent us from experiencing victory.

That includes keeping us from understanding, embracing, and unleashing our unique identity.

Scripture says it this way: "Be alert and of sober mind. Your enemy the devil prowls around like a roaring lion looking for someone to devour" (1 Peter 5:8). The apostle Paul told the church in Ephesus, "Our struggle is not against flesh and blood, but against the rulers, against the authorities, against the powers of this dark world and against the spiritual forces of evil in the heavenly realms" (Ephesians 6:12).

I don't want to make any assumptions about your spiritual beliefs, but I do want you to know the reality of your situation. It's true that you have a unique identity given to you by your Creator. It's also true that you have an enemy at work who you do not see, and that enemy does not want you to fully embrace who God called you to be. I'm talking about the enemy of God, the enemy of your soul, and the enemy of your purpose.

HURTS, HOLES, AND HAZARDS

I know we've covered a lot of ground in this chapter, but I want to end with some practical things you can do. I want to show you how to start identifying the specific obstacles that may be hindering you from embracing your unique identity. As we've seen, these obstacles can be emotional, relational, cultural, and spiritual—but they're not going to be neat and clean. Everything will be mixed and mashed together in a way that makes it difficult to discern what's going on.

So I'm going to ask you three questions that I've found

to be helpful not only in identifying the obstacles but also in resolving them.

Here's the first question: *Where is the hurt?* By "hurt," I mean something that was done to you that shouldn't have been done to you. You were injured by something that actively caused you harm, and that injury was never resolved. Remember, it's common for us to push down or ignore emotional wounds until it seems like they go away—but they never actually go away. They just keep hurting.

So where are the hurts in your life? Where have you sustained internal wounds that have never healed? Take a moment to think about that question, and then write down your answers in the space below.

_____

_____

_____

Here's the second question: *Where are the holes?* By "holes," I mean something that should have been done for you but was not done. This is the inverse of our hurts. All of us have basic needs that should be met by our caregivers—physical, emotional, and spiritual. When those needs are not met, it creates a hole. Another kind of wound.

What about you? Where have you been neglected or ignored? What have you always longed to receive but never received? Where are you leaking right now from the inside out? You can't move forward until those holes are patched up, so take a moment to identify them below:

_____

_____

_____

_____

Here's the final question: *Where are the hazards?* By "hazards," I mean the situations or circumstances that keep tripping you up in life. These aren't onetime incidents where you made a mistake and learned your lesson. No, hazards are those issues that keep coming up. And they keep getting in the way of your hopes and dreams.

A hazard could be an addiction in your life—a need for something you are unable to control. A hazard could be a habit or a series of routines that continually causes trouble—overeating when you're upset, for example, or running away from relationships when someone gets too close.

Where are your hazards? Answer that question honestly, and write down your responses below.

_____

_____

_____

_____

Hurts, holes, and hazards are all indicators that something is wrong in our lives. They are like markers that show us where we've been wounded. Where we are carrying soul wounds.

Once you identify those markers, the next step is to do something about it. Talk with someone. Pray and seek the prayers of others. Join a group or a program. Visit a counselor. There are all kinds of options, and there are all sorts of pathways toward healing.

But know this. Healing doesn't happen until you take action, until you make new choices. And without healing, you will have a difficult time identifying and removing the obstacles that are hindering you from being the person you were created to be and achieving all you were created to achieve.

CHAPTER 7

DETERMINE TO MOVE FORWARD

Have you ever gotten stuck while driving? No matter whether you're in mud or snow, the results are the same. You press the gas and hear the revving of the engine, but the tires just spin. You turn the steering wheel back and forth, trying to find some kind of traction. But the tires just spin again. You don't go anywhere. In fact, spinning those tires just digs you in deeper.

I know some people who feel compelled to try to push their car out in such situations. They put their shoulder up against the bumper and heave. Then they heave again, trying to rock the car back and forth until some kind of momentum is generated and some type of forward progress can be made.

But it's useless. Unless you're Dwayne "The Rock" Johnson, you're *not* pushing a two-ton automobile out of a rut. It just doesn't happen.

You're stuck.

I hate being stuck because it makes me feel frustrated. I have places to go and things to do, but I'm wasting time trying to extricate myself from a situation I did not foresee. I also hate being stuck because it makes me feel helpless. It forces me to admit the reality that there are some problems I cannot solve on my own.

In my experience, the only way to get unstuck is to apply the proper tools to the job. The best-case scenario is for you to have a Triple-A card in your wallet or purse, which means you can have a tow truck sent to your location and quickly resolve your situation. Lacking that, a winch can pull you out. Or if you're desperate, it's possible to wedge a two-by-four or something similar under one of the tires so it can stop spinning and gain traction.

I bring this up because I know many people feel like their wheels are spinning when it comes to their lives. They keep pressing the gas, trying to get something going—but nothing happens. They're stuck.

Maybe you've lived through one of those seasons. Maybe you're living in the middle of such a season now. Maybe that's why you're reading this book.

We've been focused on the importance of embracing our unique identity in recent chapters—of learning to accept and value who we were created to be so we can do what we were created to do. In the previous chapter, we explored several obstacles that prevent people from embracing their unique identity. These obstacles often start with emotional issues. Relational and cultural obstacles drag us down, and spiritual obstacles are thrown in our path by a spiritual enemy.

All of these things contribute to that feeling of being stuck, of spinning our wheels and going nowhere, even though we desperately desire to live a life of purpose and meaning.

In this chapter, I'll give you several tools to get yourself unstuck. It's easy to stay in the car and keep hitting that gas pedal—keep spinning those wheels. Yet neither you nor I will make any progress toward our purpose and calling until we decide to make progress.

Until we determine to move forward.

FIGHT FOR HEALING

The world has been thinking a lot about illnesses and wellness in recent years because of the COVID-19 pandemic. I have no interest in getting into all that, because I'm sure you're as tired of that conversation as I am. But the pandemic has reinforced my belief in an important principle—namely, that you and I can easily catch sickness, but we will never catch health.

You know what I'm talking about, right? Sickness is passive, just like mediocrity. But health is active, just like excellence. It requires effort.

We talked about soul wounds in the previous chapter— the injuries and hurts that hit us at the foundation of who we are. You and I didn't ask for those wounds. You and I didn't go looking for emotional or relational trauma, but it happened. We've all experienced those hurts, and we all carry those wounds.

But here's what I need you to understand. You will keep carrying your soul wounds until you decide to do something about it. Until you choose to fight for healing. Because you don't catch health.

This is important. If there isn't intentionality when it comes to identifying and addressing the issues you're carrying—the harms, holes, and hazards—then those issues will continue to impact your life. They will continue to hinder your ability to understand and embrace who you really are.

When I say "fight for healing," I mean exactly that. You have to fight. You have to get large. You have to be willing to stand your ground and mix it up and keep on swinging until the wounds are addressed and you begin the process of recovering from the damage they have caused—the damage they are still causing.

Remember, you have an enemy. There are spiritual forces at work in your life that are both malignant and intelligent, forces that actively want you to remain wounded, to be prevented from embracing your unique identity so that you will never get anywhere close to achieving your unique destiny.

You have to fight for healing if you want to move forward.

So that's the first thing I want you to contemplate as you prepare not only to embrace your unique identity but to unleash it: *doing so will take action and intentionality.*

You have to fight for healing if you want to move forward.

FORGIVE GENEROUSLY

Right about now you may be thinking, *I'm willing to fight, Dharius. I'm ready to mix it up so I can stop spinning my wheels. What's next? What do I actually do?*

The answer may surprise you: forgive.

Forgiveness is the first step to healing emotional wounds and removing the relational, cultural, and spiritual obstacles that are blocking you from living out who you are. But not "forgiveness" in a general sense, as in choosing to forgive someone who took your parking spot or ate the last crescent roll at Thanksgiving dinner.

No, I'm talking about *radical forgiveness*. Choosing to forgive regularly and generously.

I have struggled with this issue myself. As a pastor and disciple of Jesus, I have known about the importance of forgiveness for a long time. I've preached dozens of messages on those Scripture passages where God *requires*—not suggests, but requires—his followers to forgive those who harm them.

Jesus said it plainly: "For if you forgive other people when they sin against you, your heavenly Father will also forgive you. But if you do not forgive others their sins, your Father will not forgive your sins" (Matthew 6:14-15).

Even as a coach and a counselor, I have seen the way unforgiveness harms people—the way it burns and festers inside those who refuse to forgive others. I've seen it for decades. Have you ever heard someone say, "Unforgiveness is like drinking poison and waiting for the other person to die"? It's true. I've known that for a long time.

Still, despite my knowledge about the importance of forgiveness and my own experiences watching other people suffer because of their unforgiveness, I found myself some years back struggling with an inability to forgive. For a long time I had been carrying deep wounds connected to my family. I knew there was resentment in my heart. Bitterness. Unforgiveness. I wanted to release those things. I wanted to forgive and find healing.

But I couldn't.

I recognized the need for forgiveness, yet I was having trouble choosing to forgive in a way that actually stuck—in a way that mattered and made it possible to heal.

So I saw a counselor, and we talked about it. One of the first things she said to me was profound. "Dharius," she said, "you can't do forgiveness right if you understand it wrong."

Which is true about most important things in life, right? When we don't have a proper understanding of what something is, we can't effectively incorporate that something into our lives.

As we continued to talk, this counselor walked me through three *p*'s to help me get a better understanding of what forgiveness is so I could choose to forgive in a way that was effectual.

See Forgiveness as a Pardon

The first thing the counselor said is that we need to see forgiveness as a *pardon*, which is an important term. It's a legal term. Specifically, the dictionary defines a pardon as "a release from the legal penalties of an offense." Or when we use pardon as a verb, it means "to absolve from the consequences of a fault or crime."

The key words there are *release* and *absolve*. Forgiveness means releasing those who have harmed us. It means letting go. It means setting someone free.

Over the years, I've come to understand that the hurts and the harms we receive from others can never be repaid. Those wrongs cannot be made right. That's true even if the other party apologizes. That's true even if the other party feels really bad and truly regrets what they did to you. That's true even if the person who harmed you changes their behavior and treats you in ways that are astronomically and exponentially better than what they did to harm you.

Even if all that is true, it's still not going to make up for the damage you experienced. It's still not going to make up for the nights of sleep you lost. Why? Because nothing can change what happened in the past. When someone injures you at the level of a soul wound, they cannot give you back what they took.

Therefore, your only way forward is to pardon those people and what they did. Release them from liability. Absolve them from their consequences. You have to write off those experiences as bad debt that you refuse to carry one step farther.

Importantly, that is the picture of forgiveness we see in the Bible: "As far as the east is from the west, so far has [God] removed our transgressions from us" (Psalm 103:12).

You and I need to see forgiveness as a pardon in order for us to forgive in a way that matters.

See Forgiveness as a Process

The second thing to recognize is that forgiveness is a *process*. This is where many of us fail to experience the power of true forgiveness.

Most of us think of forgiveness as a onetime decision. Right? We think of forgiveness in terms of a moment—a single event. We found the person who hurt us, looked them in the eye, and said, "I forgive you." That's what forgiveness means to most people. Therefore, most people expect that single act of verbalization to bring to an end the harm they've experienced and propel them on in the journey toward healing.

They say, "I'm sorry"; you say, "I forgive you." And that's that. Time to move on.

In reality, the act of forgiving someone is not a single moment, but a process. Forgiveness is an action we have to keep taking and a choice we keep making over and over again. It's something that requires time and patience and perseverance.

Jesus spoke to this issue as well. Remember when Peter asked him about forgiveness? "Lord, how many times shall I forgive my brother or sister who sins against me? Up to seven times?" Jesus answered in a way that was shocking then and remains shocking now: "I tell you, not seven times, but seventy-seven times" (Matthew 18:21–22).

Most people interpret that passage to mean that God wants us to forgive several different types of offenses. If your brother or sister wrongs you in seventy-seven ways, you keep on forgiving them for each of those separate acts of harm. And that's certainly true and certainly helpful.

But I think there's another way to understand Jesus' words that is equally powerful and perhaps even more radical. There are times when we need to continually forgive a person for the same offense. In other words, forgiving generously means choosing and rechoosing to forgive someone over and over for each time they wounded you.

> **Forgiving generously means choosing and rechoosing to forgive someone.**

Let's go back to the previous example in which your father left your home when you were young, which caused a soul wound. His absence and lack of care created a hole in your heart that has been leaking for years. In order to begin healing that wound and removing that emotional obstacle from your life, you need to forgive your dad. You need to reach out to him if possible, admit to the hurt he caused, and then verbally express your decision to forgive him. To pardon him from any liability.

But that's just the beginning. Why? Because there are going to be instances in which you receive new information or experience new consequences that are connected to your father's absence.

Let's say you take a DNA test and realize you have siblings out there you never knew existed. That's new information connected to your soul wound. And even if that wound has begun to heal—even if you were genuine in your desire to forgive your father—that new information can rip everything open again.

It can start the hurting once more. So you need to once again make the choice to forgive generously.

Or let's say you just experienced the wonderous birth of your own child. Now you are a parent. Now you are the one responsible for this little life. What's going to happen? The pain of your father's absence, the harm of his decision to leave, will create new consequences in your life. Each time you engage with your child, there's the possibility you'll be triggered once more by the consequences of your daddy's decision to leave.

What can you do? Forgive generously. Keep forgiving over and over again, even if you are forgiving the same person for the same offense. Even if you have to do it seventy-seven times a day, keep choosing to forgive.

Because forgiveness is a process.

See Forgiveness as the Path to Healing

The final *p* my counselor pointed me to was to show me that forgiveness is the *path to healing*. Not *a* path, but *the* path. Forgiveness is the only prescription for resolving the hurts and harms we are carrying. And resolving these hurts and harms is a necessary element for our embracing of our unique identity.

What do I mean when I say forgiveness is the path to healing? First, we need to understand what happens when people hurt us. Because what happens to us is often overshadowed by what happens inside us.

When we experience harm (something bad done to us) or we experience a hole (something good withheld from us), those moments change us. Specifically, they cause a buildup of negative emotions. I'm talking about anger. Resentment. Bitterness. The desire for revenge.

The collateral damage of the pain we experience gets condensed into emotional baggage that stays with us. It weighs us down, whether we realize we're carrying it or not. Moving on from whatever hurt us doesn't remove that baggage. Imagine you grew up with a sibling who physically tried to hurt you. They hit you and pushed you down, maybe because of their own sense of inadequacy. That hurt creates a problem inside of you. Something you have to carry and deal with. And that problem doesn't go away simply because your sibling figures out their junk and stops trying to hurt you.

I wish the absence of pain were enough to solve the consequences of pain, but it isn't. Even if your sibling beat you down for two years and then spent four years working to be extra nice to you as a way to make up for things, the problem still wouldn't be solved. You would still carry that emotional baggage of feeling wronged. Of being violated. You would still carry that anger and fear.

If someone steals money from you, things don't get solved internally even if you recover the money. You are still carrying the emotional baggage of feeling wronged. Of being violated. You are still carrying that anger and fear.

Forgiveness is the only way to release that emotional baggage. It's the only direction that allows you to not only resolve an issue in a legal or moral sense but also heal from the internal consequences of that issue on an emotional level.

Forgiveness is the path to healing.

FIND YOURSELF IN SCRIPTURE AND IN HISTORY

Time to pivot a little bit.

We've been exploring how to move past the different obstacles that keep us from embracing our unique identity.

We do that first by actively fighting to be healed from those obstacles, and second by intentionally choosing to offer generous forgiveness to those who have wounded us in ways that put those obstacles in our path.

Now let's look at some tools that help us do the work of embracing who we were created to be and what we were created to do. To do that, I want us to start thinking less in terms of "what" and more in terms of "who."

Here's a principle that reflects what I mean. *In order for us to be who we are called and created to be, we need more than information; we need examples.*

There comes a time on our journey toward living out our true selves when words become less and less helpful. Teaching becomes less and less helpful. In those moments, what we often need are pictures. We need templates to follow. We need examples of women and men who have already done what we want to do so we can follow them in our journey toward becoming who we are.

In my experience, two of the best places to find these examples are in Scripture and in history.

Find Yourself in Scripture

The author of the book of Hebrews had a goal that in many ways is similar to my goal for writing this book. Specifically, the writer of this letter was trying to help people change their way of thinking so they could change the way they viewed themselves at the core. In his case, he wrote to Jewish Christians in the early church to urge them to stop thinking of themselves in the "old" ways connected to the sacrificial system and start thinking of themselves in a "new" way connected to faith in Jesus Christ.

That was a big ask! The writer's audience was steeped in

thousands of years of tradition, and he was undertaking the task of revealing Jesus' identity as the Messiah—as the fulfillment of those thousands of years of ritual and teaching and tradition.

One of the ways the author of Hebrews sought to accomplish that goal was by exhorting his readers to follow the example of those who had gone before: "We do not want you to become lazy, but to imitate those who through faith and patience inherit what has been promised" (6:12). Later in that same epistle, he worked his way through a whole list of people to show his readers how to live by faith. We call it the "Hall of Faith" today.

> By faith Abel brought God a better offering than Cain did. By faith he was commended as righteous, when God spoke well of his offerings. And by faith Abel still speaks, even though he is dead.
>
> By faith Enoch was taken from this life, so that he did not experience death: "He could not be found, because God had taken him away." For before he was taken, he was commended as one who pleased God. And without faith it is impossible to please God, because anyone who comes to him must believe that he exists and that he rewards those who earnestly seek him.
>
> By faith Noah, when warned about things not yet seen, in holy fear built an ark to save his family. By his faith he condemned the world and became heir of the righteousness that is in keeping with faith. (11:4–7)

That's just a small sample of the chapter, but you can see what the author was doing, right? *Noah was a man who lived by faith, and you can see it when he did this. Abraham lived by faith, and here are all the ways it came to expression in his actions. Jacob, Joseph, Moses, Rahab, Samson, Gideon—they all demonstrated faith in these ways, and you can demonstrate faith by emulating their lives.*

You and I are in the same boat as the readers in the early church. We need examples because much of what it means to live out our unique identity needs to be caught rather than taught.

One of the ways you can actively embrace your unique identity is to look for people in Scripture you resonate with in a special way. Look for men and women in God's Word who were built like you. Look for men and women in Scripture who did the kinds of things you want to do.

Remember, the "characters" in God's Word were not characters like Luke Skywalker or Black Panther. They were real people with real lives and real flaws. They made mistakes. Many of them did stupid things. Yet many of them also changed the world. As they reached out to God and began to understand not just *how* he made them but *why* he made them, those women and men achieved incredible things.

You can follow a similar path by finding yourself in their lives.

To give you an example, I have a special connection with the apostle Paul. I resonate with Paul because he was an entrepreneur. Like me. Paul traveled all over the world, preaching the gospel and planting churches, but he financed those efforts by sewing and selling tents. He had business awareness and acumen.

Another reason I gravitate toward Paul as an example is the way he navigated multiple arenas and multiple contexts. When Paul was in Jerusalem, he spoke to the Jewish people with a keen awareness of the context of their ancient traditions and sacred texts. When Paul was in Athens at the Areopagus, he quoted Greek philosophy. When Paul was in Rome, he demonstrated practical knowledge of his rights as a Roman citizen, and he used those rights to maximum effect.

Reading about the way Paul operated with such ease in multiple contexts inspired me. It gave me a picture of what I could do in my culture and my contexts.

You can experience something similar when you find yourself in Scripture.

I don't know your story, but let's say you grew up with many gifts. You had a lot of support and a large number of people who were pulling for you—people who invested in you because they saw your potential. Yet all these years later, you're still trying to realize that potential. You're still trying to figure things out. If so, I recommend you find yourself in Scripture and connect with King Saul. Study his story and see if you can determine some of the short circuits that derailed his potential. You have the opportunity to avoid his mistakes.

Or maybe you've been functioning for years as a cog in the machine. You're good at your job, and people generally respect you as a person. Even as a leader. Still, you know the people you spend time with each day are ruthless. They may like you, but they don't care about you—and they will step on top of you to get ahead. If that sounds familiar, you have a great opportunity to find yourself in Scripture by studying the life of Daniel.

Find Yourself in History

One of the helpful movements that has come out of the business space in recent decades has been the renewed appreciation in our culture for mentorships. Both leaders and would-be leaders have rediscovered the value of connecting with others in the context of teaching and training relationships.

I have benefited from wonderful mentors in the different contexts of my different professions, and I still seek out these types of relationships today. But I've also come to understand that mentorship doesn't have to occur through the vehicle of relationship. It's both possible and incredibly helpful to follow a mentor or a teacher you've never met—even one you couldn't possibly meet on this side of eternity.

That's what I mean when I talk about finding yourself in history. You can have a real, special, meaningful, productive connection with a historical figure simply by reading what they wrote, listening to what they said, and learning about what they did.

Pay attention to that last one, because it's important. The people who become known in history are often remembered for big things. They started a revolution, for example, or a movement, or they achieved something that was magnificent. That's what we see when we take a broad look at history—those public accomplishments.

What we don't see is all the private work that had to take place in order to make those public accomplishments possible. I've said before that I could do my very best to emulate Michael Jordan on the basketball court. I could stick my tongue out when dribbling up the court. I could do my best impression of MJ's fadeaway jumper. (Unfortunately, I can't duplicate his height of six feet six.) The problem is that trying to emulate Air Jordan's public game wouldn't get me far unless I was willing to emulate his private practice—to put in hundreds of hours shooting thousands of shots over and over again.

So finding yourself in history allows you to study people who were successful and learn *why* they were successful. It lets you not only hear their words but also imitate their actions.

I'll give you an example. One of the people I resonate with from history is Charles Spurgeon. If you don't know that name, Spurgeon was a major force in the church in Great Britain during the nineteenth century. He was a pastor of an influential church in London, but he was also a writer who blessed many people with his words. In fact, Spurgeon was so beloved that when he died in 1892, more than a hundred thousand people lined the streets of London to watch his body on parade from the church to the cemetery.

Study people who were successful and learn _why_ they were successful.

I resonated with Charles Spurgeon because he was one of the first examples I encountered of a thinking pastor. What we might call a pastor-theologian today. I liked the time and attention he gave to creating content. No doubt Spurgeon was a powerful preacher, and people came from around the world to hear him speak. But he also spent time honing his thoughts and his mind, which allowed him to craft words in ways that even today are considered extraordinary.

Reading Spurgeon's writings and studying his life helped me see that serving God as a pastor didn't have to entail being in meetings all day. I didn't have to give a major portion of my time to budget planning or capital campaigns—other people are gifted in those areas, and it's okay that I'm not. Frankly, Spurgeon inspired me even in his death because his example galvanized a conviction that when I'm no longer here, I will have cared way more about leaving people with words to live by than buildings to sit in.

Myles Munroe is another of my mentors whom I have never met. He is someone from history who has helped me better understand the person I was created to be and the work I was created to do. And I especially resonated with Myles because he lived and worked during my lifetime. He died several years ago in a plane crash, but before that I could watch him and learn about him in real time.

Just to give you a sense of the man, let me share a quick story about Myles that most people haven't heard. He grew up and ministered in the Bahamas—which meant he started to be sought out by several of the celebrities and public figures who had vacation homes in the Bahamas. One celebrity in particular was having marital trouble that was receiving public attention. He was an athlete, and he got in touch with Myles to ask for help. So Myles visited the couple in their home several times for marriage counseling.

One day as Myles was leaving, this multimillion-dollar, multitalented athlete stopped the pastor at the door. "Myles," he said, "you've been coming to the house so much and you won't take any money. What can we give you? At least let me sign something for your kids."

Myles Munroe just shook his head. "No, thank you," he said. "You need what I have way more than I need what you have."

Wow! I love that story. I love that kind of confidence and clarity and conviction. I want to present myself like that in the world, and it's one of the reasons I resonated so deeply when I began to discover Myles Munroe and read and listen to everything he had to say.

Myles was one of the first pastoral leaders I was exposed to who was successfully adding value in both the church world and the business space. Like the apostle Paul, Myles Munroe was comfortable in several contexts. He's one of the only people I know who could be preaching in church one day, be on the stage with Les Brown the next day, and then fly out to do a leadership training session for the British Parliament the day after that.

My journey of understanding who Myles Munroe was helped me *understand* who I am. Not only that, but he helped me *embrace* who I am because he showed me it was possible to live the life I wanted to live and achieve the kind of influence I wanted to achieve. Even though I never met this man, he helped validate the truth that what I have to share is valuable and needed outside the walls of the church.

You can experience that same kind of benefit and blessing when you find yourself in Scripture and in history. And by doing so, you will have more opportunities to embrace your unique identity.

FORGE YOUR TRIBE

I want to add one more tool to your toolbox. In order to move forward, forge yourself a tribe. By "tribe," I mean a community of people whose giftings and goals are similar to your own and who are serious about living lives of meaning and purpose.

Now when I use the word *community*, I want to make it clear that I'm not talking about the kind of Christian community we typically associate with church congregations, Sunday school classes, or small groups. Don't get me wrong, those communities are important. And certainly it's possible to find and forge your tribe within the context of a church. But what I'm talking about is something different.

One of the points I've been hammering throughout these pages is that you are unique. There is nobody exactly like you in the world—nobody with your specific design, your specific mix of gifts, and your specific mission to contribute to human flourishing in your specific way. You are one of a kind.

But there are people who are *similar* to you. People with

similar design and similar dreams. People whose mix of gifts may overlap with your own in several ways. And people who are seeking to make *their* difference for the same reasons—and perhaps even in the same way—as you are seeking to make *your* difference.

Those are the people you need to find for your tribe. Why? Because you can help one another. You can push one another. You can teach one another. You can support one another. And you can correct one another *when*—not if—you or others start to drift off course.

I use the word *forge* because, once again, this is a step that requires intentionality. And I know the benefit of being intentional in this area because this is an area in which I struggled for many years.

There was a long time when I felt almost desperate to find my tribe. I knew there were people out there who had gifts and goals similar to my own. I had encountered such people every now and then at conferences and other venues. But those encounters were few and far between, and those relationships were undeveloped.

Once I did begin to connect more regularly and more deeply with people who understood my goals, I quickly realized I had been missing an important piece of my development. I had been missing a crucial tool in my toolbox, and I never wanted to be without that tool again.

Here's what I'll tell you about having a tribe. For me personally, I have felt much less weird than I used to feel. I also feel much more supported, both personally and professionally. And I feel affirmed in my assignment because I see the fruitfulness of other people who are a little farther along than I am.

I want the same for you.

Maybe you're wondering, *What was the problem, Dharius?*

What kept you from enjoying that kind of tribe for so many years?
The answer: I was waiting for God to deliver my tribe to my
doorstep like some kind of divine order from Amazon.com.
I was idle, expecting my people to come to me. And that strat-
egy didn't work.

The alternative is to go out and create the kind of commu-
nity you need. Swords don't just happen by accident. Neither
do necklaces or doorknobs or any other item made up of pre-
cision parts. They all need to be forged. They all need to be
actively and intentionally crafted.

The same is true for your tribe. You need to go out and
find the people who can help you embrace who you are and
keep you moving forward as you strive to make your ultimate
contribution to human flourishing.

Where do I see me?
In scripture or history?

PART 3

UNLEASH

CHAPTER 8

TAKE YOUR SHOT

It's one of the best-known stories ever. Not just in the Bible, but ever. In all of human history. People have been telling this story for thousands of years, and they'll continue telling it for thousands more.

I'm talking about David versus Goliath.

In case it's been a while since you read that story, let me highlight the key moment for you. It's recorded in the book of 1 Samuel. Here we go:

> Meanwhile, the Philistine, with his shield bearer in front of him, kept coming closer to David. He looked David over and saw that he was little more than a boy, glowing with health and handsome, and he despised him. He said to David, "Am I a dog, that you come at me with sticks?" And the Philistine cursed David by his gods. "Come here," he said, "and I'll give your flesh to the birds and the wild animals!"
>
> David said to the Philistine, "You come against me with sword and spear and javelin, but I come against you

in the name of the LORD Almighty, the God of the armies of Israel, whom you have defied. This day the LORD will deliver you into my hands, and I'll strike you down and cut off your head. This very day I will give the carcasses of the Philistine army to the birds and the wild animals, and the whole world will know that there is a God in Israel. All those gathered here will know that it is not by sword or spear that the LORD saves; for the battle is the LORD's, and he will give all of you into our hands."

As the Philistine moved closer to attack him, David ran quickly away from the battle line to avoid a conflict. Reaching into his bag, he put away his sling. Then he walked away from both armies without a word.

So David refused his moment. He chose the safest path possible and returned meekly to his father's sheep. (1 Samuel 17:41–50)

Oh, wait, did that story end a little differently from what you remember? Yes, I doctored those final two paragraphs a little bit. What I wrote is a hypothetical example of how that story might have played out if David had decided not to fight.

It's a little shocking to read, isn't it? David's story has been so ingrained in our lives that any alterations are strange. Almost offensive. But it's precisely because that story is so ubiquitous in our experience that I think it deserves to be considered from some different angles.

Think specifically about the moment David unleashed his stone against Goliath. I'm sure it only took a few seconds, so try to play it back in slow motion in your mind.

Scripture says David was "the youngest" of Jesse's sons when this battle took place (1 Samuel 17:14). A teenager. So imagine his smooth-cheeked face staring calmly as his slender fingers choose a stone from his pouch. Imagine his curly hair spilling over his neck. The wiry body of a young man still working to get comfortable in his own skin.

Now imagine Goliath. The giant. Can you hear the sound of his armor clanking as he marches slowly and methodically toward the boy? Can you see the hatred in his eyes and the spittle caught up in his beard? Can you smell the stench in his clothes from a hundred marches and a hundred battles and thousands of fallen enemies tossed cruelly to the dusty ground? This is the enemy. The unstoppable force that must be stopped.

Here comes the moment. I picture Goliath marching implacably toward the boy. A straight line the shortest distance between two points. No dodging, just the approach of death.

I picture David swinging the sling above his head. His eyes are fixed on Goliath, and his head doesn't move even as his shoulder whips his wrist and hand around again and again. There is a slight whooshing sound in the air as the leather cord whistles in its repeated orbit. Then it happens. A flex of David's knees. A twist of the hips. A Patrick Mahomes–like extension of David's right arm as he scythes forward with the sling.

Nobody sees the stone. It's too fast. But everybody hears the impact—everybody except Goliath, whose lights have already been turned out. The giant's body stiffens, his momentum stopped. His legs wobble once. Twice. Then he falls with the clattering clash of expensive armor smashing into dirt.

Victory.

Why do I highlight this particular event? Because that was the moment everything changed in David's life. Really, it was the moment everything changed for Israel as a nation. Everything in David's life leading up to that moment had been preparation. The years in his father's house. The thousands of rugged hours living out with the flocks. Deepening his relationship with God through worship and praise.

Everything in David's past and everything in David's future hinged on that one instant. On that one choice. Would he unleash the stone? Or would he turn and walk away?

In a similar way, everything you've covered in this book so far has been a type of preparation. In part 1, you worked to *understand* the concept of *unique identity* and how it applies to your purpose. You've explored your *unique design, unique discontent, unique dreams,* and *unique destiny.* In part 2, you took the next step of *embracing* your unique identity, which means not just accepting the reality that you are unique and your difference is your superpower but also valuing who you are. Treasuring your you-ness.

Now it's time to *unleash* your unique identity. To learn what it's like to get in the game. Practice is over, and now the time has come to take your shot for real.

There's a key question to consider as we work through this chapter together—namely, what does it take for a person such as you or me to unleash our unique identity? What does it take for a person to stop contemplating and start doing?

I want to give you four answers to those questions. It takes *calling.* It takes *courage.* It takes *competency.* And it takes *calculation.* We'll explore each of these concepts through David's story.

IT TAKES CALLING

You may be wondering what I mean by the word *unleash.* That's fair. Nobody is carrying slings around these days, and none of us are going to do any good by throwing stones in our communities. So what exactly should we be unleashing?

The short answer is *yourself.* Your *unique identity.* That's what you need to unleash. Throughout these pages, we've focused on the truth that you have a unique identity. That you were created and designed intentionally to be different from every other person. There is no one like you, and your Creator did that on purpose. That's the reality.

To *unleash* your unique identity is to live out that reality. It means acting on what you've *understood* and *embraced* about yourself—that you are unique, and that your uniqueness is the key to a life of meaning. It means making choices that are consistent with who you know yourself to be rather than who or what everybody around you expects you to be.

That's unleashing your unique identity. It's living fully out of who you are.

Now it's important to remember that your identity is composed of two halves—both of which stem from the fact that you are the product of your Creator. The first is *who you were created to be,* and the second is *what you were created to do.* These two halves can be boiled down to two words you can find all throughout this book: *calling* and *purpose.*

Let's start with the concept of calling by exploring the specific and verbal calling David received from God:

> The LORD said to Samuel, "How long will you mourn for Saul, since I have rejected him as king over Israel? Fill your horn with oil and be on your way; I am sending you to Jesse of Bethlehem. I have chosen one of his sons to be king." . . .
>
> Then Jesse called Abinadab and had him pass in front of Samuel. But Samuel said, "The LORD has not chosen this one either." Jesse then had Shammah pass by, but Samuel said, "Nor has the LORD chosen this one." Jesse had seven of his sons pass before Samuel, but Samuel said to him,

"The LORD has not chosen these." So he asked Jesse, "Are these all the sons you have?"

"There is still the youngest," Jesse answered. "He is tending the sheep."

Samuel said, "Send for him; we will not sit down until he arrives."

So he sent for him and had him brought in. He was glowing with health and had a fine appearance and handsome features.

Then the LORD said, "Rise and anoint him; this is the one."

So Samuel took the horn of oil and anointed him in the presence of his brothers, and from that day on the Spirit of the LORD came powerfully upon David. Samuel then went to Ramah. (1 Samuel 16:1, 8–13)

A little context here. Saul was Israel's first king, but he had rejected God on several occasions. As a result, God sent Samuel the prophet to anoint a new king—really, a new lineage of kings. Families were very hierarchical in the ancient world, with the oldest son typically awarded the best of everything. David was the youngest son, which meant when a prophet showed up to bless one of Jesse's children, nobody even thought to call in David from the fields. Nobody expected anything from David.

But God knew better.

Here's what was happening in that passage. God was letting David know who he was. He was telling David about himself.

Notice that nothing changed about David's external circumstances. He was still the youngest son, which meant he still went out into the fields day after day and night after night to watch his father's sheep. He still dressed in the same way. He still ate the same food. He still experienced the same disrespect and bullying from his brothers. In most of the ways that mattered, nothing had changed.

Except that David now understood his identity. He wasn't a shepherd. He wasn't a lowly seventh son. He wasn't a lonely youth who should be thankful for any potential bride—if his father ever got around to arranging a marriage for him.

No, David was a king. That was his calling.

Importantly, God still calls his people today. Does he do so verbally and symbolically, as he did with David through the prophet Samuel? Sometimes, but it's rare. Does God call us to specific vocations or positions, as he did with David when he declared him the next king? Again the answer is sometimes, but most often not.

In the majority of cases today, God helps us understand who we are through the voice of his Spirit, through the words of Scripture, through the counsel of others we trust, and through our own personal experiences and reflections. God calls us today by helping us recognize the distinctive elements of our design. He calls us through our unique discontent and our unique dreams. And he calls us by planting a vision in our hearts of the ultimate contribution he has designed us to make toward human flourishing. It is my very sincere hope that God has used the pages of this book to advance that calling in your mind and heart—to tell you who you are.

All of these options are ways that God activates us as his people. In many ways, our *calling* is the first step in our commission to do the work God created us to do.

That brings us to *purpose*. I define it as *the reason for the creation or existence of a thing*. Nothing in our universe is random. Our Creator doesn't work that way. Instead, every element of creation has a distinct purpose—a distinct reason for its existence.

Including you and me.

Importantly, the reason something gets created is almost always connected to problems. That's easy to see through human acts of creation. Humanity needed a way to breach the atmosphere and explore the surface of the moon, so we created rocket boosters. Those boosters had (and still have) a specific purpose. When a construction crew has a problem with concrete flowing outside the boundaries of where they want it to go, they create forms that keep everything in its proper place while the concrete dries.

To say that you and I are created with a purpose means our creation is connected to problems as well. Here's a principle: *Your purpose, when properly fulfilled, will contribute solutions to some of the problems that exist in your day.* Remember the main idea behind unique discontent? The problems that bother you most are likely the problems you were created to solve.

> **Your purpose, when properly fulfilled, will contribute solutions to some of the problems that exist in your day.**

That's purpose. You were created for a reason. Just like David.

So the act of *unleashing* your unique identity means living in the light of your calling and purpose. It's more than *understanding* a concept (although that's important). It's more than *embracing* your value (although that's important too). It means daily choosing to live in a way that is consistent with who you were created to be and what you were created to do.

I can picture a barista at one of our local coffee shops who stands at the counter with confidence every single day. In her mind, she is not making coffee. She's not even making a few bucks. She has a calling to serve people and bless those who show up in her world each day—which means she is making her difference. She is unleashing her unique identity by living out her calling.

You and I have the same opportunity, no matter what our individual calling may be.

One more thought before we move to the next section. Back in chapter 4 we talked about the concept of *unique destiny*. This is your ultimate contribution to human flourishing. It's your legacy. In many ways, your destiny is the ultimate expression of your calling and purpose. Importantly, though, we saw that most people achieve and experience their unique destiny in a specific season of their lives. It's not an "everyday thing."

What I want you to see right now, however, is that calling and purpose are very much everyday things. Every morning when you wake up, you can be certain that you will be presented with multiple opportunities to live out your calling and purpose—multiple opportunities to unleash your unique identity. In other words, you have opportunities every day to address in real ways the problems you were created to address. To make your difference in the world.

Here's the good news. The more consistent we are in engaging those opportunities and the more intentional we are about living authentically every moment of our lives, the faster we will reach our unique destiny and the larger our legacy will become.

IT TAKES COURAGE

Because we are working through these concepts in a step-by-step fashion, it may sound like all of this is easy. *Understand who I am. Okay. Value my uniqueness. Check. Make choices each day that are consistent with my calling and purpose. Got it.*

Unleashing your unique destiny is incredibly important, and it's necessary if you want to experience real meaning and real impact—but it's not easy. The work is hard and the risks are real, because every day you are going to deal with the increasing pressure of being who others expect you to be and doing what everyone around you expects you to do. Have you ever tried to walk against the current in a flowing river or a flooding creek? That's what it feels like to live authentically in a world built on conformity.

All of which means unleashing your unique identity takes courage. Just ask David.

There are two moments in David's life that offer us a wonderful picture of the courage it takes to unleash our unique identity. I mentioned the first at the beginning of this book, but I'd like to take a deeper look at the text:

> Then Saul dressed David in his own tunic. He put a coat of armor on him and a bronze helmet on his head. David fastened on his sword over the tunic and tried walking around, because he was not used to them.
>
> "I cannot go in these," he said to Saul, "because I am not used to them." So he took them off. Then he took his staff in his hand, chose five smooth stones from the stream, put them in the pouch of his shepherd's bag and, with his sling in his hand, approached the Philistine. (1 Samuel 17:38-40)

This is the moment in David's story that comes after David's decision to fight Goliath but before the actual battle. There is an interlude in which King Saul quizzes David about the young man's qualifications for such a fight. Then, once the king is satisfied, he prepares David by blessing him with royal equipment.

Don't miss this moment because it was a uniquely courageous act.

Saul gave David his own shirt. He called in servants and had them buckle David into the very best armor they could find and place the very best helmet over the young man's head. This was Saul extending a courtesy and a kindness to this unknown youth that the most experienced soldiers in his army likely would have killed to receive themselves. It was a huge honor.

Yet David looked into Saul's face and said, "No, thank you."

Remember, Saul was the king. And kings in the ancient world were used to getting their way and very much not used to being told no. This wasn't like complaining about your senator on social media. For David, this was a highly personal and very risky rejection of what the king had offered.

But it's more than that. Saul wasn't just a king; he was also an experienced warrior. He had fought his way through many battles. He had killed many men. And even more than that, he was in charge of the entire military. He commanded an army of thousands of soldiers, and each of those soldiers believed in their hearts that the best way to fight a giant was with the highest quality armor to protect yourself and the sharpest sword with which to attack.

In contrast, David had no military experience. He had fought no battles. He had killed no people. He was a boy, and he was a shepherd! And yet he had the courage to say, in effect, "I understand all of you do things a certain way, and I know that method has been successful in the past. But I am going to solve this problem in a way that fits who I was created to be rather than conform to what you expect me to do."

That's the kind of courage it takes to unleash your unique identity.

The second way David demonstrated courage in this story is that he was willing to engage a battle that everyone else around him was afraid to fight. Here's another look at the story:

> Goliath stood and shouted to the ranks of Israel, "Why do you come out and line up for battle? Am I not a Philistine, and are you not the servants of Saul? Choose a man and have him come down to me. If he is able to fight and kill me, we will become your subjects; but if I overcome him and kill him, you will become our subjects and serve us." Then the Philistine said, "This day I defy the armies of Israel! Give me a man and let us fight each other." On hearing the Philistine's words, Saul and all the Israelites were dismayed and terrified. (1 Samuel 17:8–11)

Everyone knew the problem. From Saul all the way down to the lowest servant in the camp, they all understood the issue that needed to be resolved. Goliath. More than that, everybody understood the solution to the problem. Someone needed to walk over to the Philistine camp and kill the giant, and then they could all go home and celebrate with the ancient Middle Eastern equivalent of fried chicken and sweet tea.

Yet according to the text, "All the Israelites were dismayed and terrified."

Except David. His choice to take up the fight required tremendous courage.

Now think of your community today. I imagine the main problems of your community are evident to most people. They are not hard to discern. And I assume most of the people who live in your community would want those problems to be solved. The question is who will have the courage to stand up and be the solution.

I know for a fact that the vast majority of people in our culture don't want other people living in poverty. Most of us are appalled at the idea of an individual or a family losing their home and being forced to live on the street. Most of us would reject the heartbreak of war and violence if we could choose to do so, and most of us would like to see healing when it comes to the political, racial, and financial divisions that have torn so many people apart.

We all see the problems. We all want solutions. Yet our world is looking desperately for those who have the courage to act in ways that can produce solutions.

It's worth asking yourself if you have that kind of mettle. That kind of bravery. And if the answer is no, it's worth finding out why.

Because it takes courage to unleash your unique identity.

IT TAKES COMPETENCY

Malcom Gladwell has a book called *David and Goliath: Underdogs, Misfits, and the Art of Battling Giants*. It's a good read, and I recommend it. Frankly, the level of research and explanation of the ancient world Gladwell was able to achieve in that book rivals most of the biblical commentaries I've read on that passage.

One of the things Gladwell focused a lot of attention on in his book and in subsequent interviews was David's sling. Here's a sample:

A slinger is someone who has a leather pouch with two long cords attached to it. And they put a projectile, either a rock or a lead ball, inside the pouch. And they whirl it around . . . and they let one of the cords go. And the effect is to send the projectile forward at—towards its target. That's what David has, and it's important to understand that that sling is not a slingshot, right? It's not a child's toy.

When David rolls it around like this, he's turning this sling around probably at six or seven revolutions per second. And that means that when the rock is released, it's going forward really fast, probably 35 meters per second. More than that, the stones in the Valley of Elah were not normal rocks. They were barium sulfate, which are rocks twice the density of normal stones. If you do the calculations on the ballistic—on the stopping power of the rock fired from David's sling, it's roughly equal to the stopping power of a 45 millimeter handgun, right? This is an incredibly devastating weapon.[1]

In addition to the sling, it's helpful to remember that David was not entirely inexperienced when it came to combat. He had not done any soldiering, but he had participated in several intense battles as the shepherd of his father's sheep— even killing lions and bears as part of that struggle.[2]

All of this tells me that David had some key competencies that made him an effective resource for God to use in a time of need. The same must be true of you and me if we want to unleash our unique identity.

When I think about this concept of competency, I picture the shepherd's bag David carried with him into battle against Goliath—a bag that contained a number of important resources to help David function well in his fight. We've already talked about the sling, and Scripture also mentioned that David stopped at a nearby stream to select five smooth stones and place them in his bag.

You and I carry our own version of a shepherd's bag as we seek to live out our unique identity. In chapter 4, we talked about three specific resources that each of us possesses: natural talents, spiritual gifts, and acquired skills. Each of those "stones" are useful as we seek to make our impact in the world.

But there are other types of resources too—other types of stones we might call *intangibles*. David's courage is a good example. It was a crucial resource for that specific moment. David also possessed a high level of physical strength, given that he was able to hurl a stone toward Goliath with the necessary velocity to knock the giant unconscious. It sounds strange, but David's youth and smaller stature were also resources in that fight, in that they caused Goliath to take David lightly and advance toward the sling with a sneer instead of a shield.

You also have a number of intangibles in your shepherd's bag of resources. Maybe you have the kind of personality that draws people in and encourages them to let down their guard. Maybe you have a brain that can remember facts with ease. Maybe you have a way with children or with animals that sets you apart. Maybe you can imitate voices or multiply large numbers in your head or operate at maximum capacity on a minimum of sleep. There's no end to the types of intangible stones we can carry in our bag.

It sounds funny to say it, but one of the ways we can identify our intangibles is to look for those areas that make us feel *weird*—that make us stick out like a sore thumb. Look at David. He was in the middle of two armies of soldiers carrying swords and shields, and yet he went out to battle with a staff and a sling. That was weird. Yet David's weirdness was part of his uniqueness, and that weirdness became a resource that contributed to his victory.

So where are you weird? What about you do others comment on or even chuckle about? What makes you different? Keep track of those traits, because they may be just what you need to get a win.

One last point on this subject. We need to recognize that part of David's effectiveness was the sharpened condition of his competencies. He hadn't allowed his talents, gifts, skills, or intangibles to grow blunt. He kept them sharp through patient practice and experience. Imagine David out there in the fields, knocking birds out of the sky with his sling. Imagine him practicing form with his staff. When a bear came and grabbed a sheep, David was ready. He knew exactly what to do because his mind and his body were sharp and ready for action. Same with Goliath. David was effective because he was ready. He was honed.

You and I must follow the same path. We won't be effective in living out our unique destiny if we allow our talents, gifts, skills, and other intangible resources to become dull through lack of use. We need to stay sharp. We need to stay alert. We need to be ready to be used when the moment of need is at hand.

IT TAKES CALCULATION

If you and I desire to unleash our unique identity and experience everything our Creator designed us to experience in this life, it's going to take both an awareness and a grabbing hold of our *calling*. It's going to take *courage* to act rather than just pondering whether to act. It's going to take *competency* as we use the talents, gifts, skills, and intangible qualities we've been given.

Finally, it's going to take *calculation*, which is the ability to count the cost and evaluate risks and rewards in light of our actions—and to do so *before* we take action. Many people refer to this ability as discernment. It's the capacity to weigh all the available options and make the right choice.

Maybe the best word to describe this quality is *wisdom*.

There are two moments in the story of David and Goliath that reveal David's wisdom—his ability to evaluate options and calculate his actions. The first is revealed in a question David asked that is often overshadowed by the action of the story. Let's take a look:

> Now the Israelites had been saying, "Do you see how this man keeps coming out? He comes out to defy Israel. The king will give great wealth to the man who kills him. He will also give him his daughter in marriage and will exempt his family from taxes in Israel."
>
> David asked the men standing near him, "What will be done for the man who kills this Philistine and removes this disgrace from Israel? Who is this uncircumcised Philistine that he should defy the armies of the living God?" (1 Samuel 17:25–26)

The setting here is important. David had been sent to the front lines by his father, not to fight, but simply to deliver supplies to his brothers and gather news to take back home. But when David saw Goliath walk into the valley and declare blasphemies against God and the armies of Israel, he got curious. He started to calculate. And he asked an important question.

"What will be done for the man who kills this Philistine and removes this disgrace from Israel?"

Am I implying that David's motives for doing battle against Goliath were greedy or grasping? No. Am I suggesting that David cared more about money and power than about the giant's affronts against God? Nope. Nor am I suggesting that David would have declined to fight Goliath if no reward had been offered. We don't know what would have happened in that hypothetical situation.

What I am saying is that David demonstrated wisdom by counting the cost before he called on the king.

Look at the situation from the lens of David's unique identity. For starters, David was bothered by Goliath's defiance of God. That's clear in his conversation with the giant at the beginning of their battle. So David experienced unique discontent when he heard the giant's rant. He was bothered, and he seemed to be bothered more than the soldiers around him.

In addition, David heard rumors about the reward that would be given to the person who defeated the giant—and clearly, that potential reward appealed to him. The possibility of marrying into the king's household stirred his unique dreams. Why? Because David had been anointed as the future king. He knew God's calling on his life. Therefore this opportunity seemed connected to his unique destiny.

Here's my point. David was being wise in calculating whether challenging the giant was the best use of unique resources in that specific moment. You and I need to demonstrate similar wisdom when it comes to unleashing our unique identity in the world.

As we've already seen, myriads of messes exist in the world today. There are a lot of problems in our communities. All of these problems need *someone* with courage and competency to step up and take action—but not all of these problems need *you* to step up. In fact, you should avoid most of these problems. Because most of the problems you encounter are not the problems you were created to solve.

Unleashing your unique identity means saying no to most things so you can say yes when it counts.

There's another part of the story in which David demonstrates wisdom. It occurs when Saul tries to give the young man his royal armor. For one thing, David was accurate in his calculations when he determined that Saul's armor was a hindrance rather than a help—that's important to note.

> **Say no to most things so you can say yes when it counts.**

But David also demonstrated wisdom in his choice of words. Look at how he answered Saul. "'I cannot go in these,' he said to Saul, 'because I am not used to them.' So he took them off" (17:39).

Notice David's candor and tact in that interaction. He did not say, "This armor isn't good enough for me." He did not say, "Only an idiot would try to fight a giant by weighing themselves down with heavy armor." Nor did David imply or sarcastically suggest that Saul should feel foolish for offering a solution that obviously wouldn't work.

No, David spoke honestly and yet kept the emphasis on himself. "*I* am not used to them."

Please allow me to speak frankly for a moment. I've noticed a high degree of arrogance in our culture over the course of my ministry, and I believe things have only ramped up to a higher degree in recent years. I see this arrogance in the church. I see it in the business arena. And I see it expressed most explicitly and harmfully on those occasions where there are multiple options for getting something done.

Many people seem to be under the impression that choosing their way of accomplishing something also means denigrating other ways of accomplishing that same task. Many people feel the need to demonize those who do things differently. They are overtly condescending to others who operate in a different way.

My brothers and sisters, this should not be.

Yes, living out of our unique identity means resisting the pressure to conform—but it also means resisting the impulse to pressure *others* to conform to *us*. Yes, there is room for critique whenever people are doing serious work. But criticism that is arrogant and unnecessary lowers the effectiveness of everyone involved.

> **We must resist the impulse to pressure *others* to conform to *us*.**

We need to be more like David. We need to unleash our unique identity with wisdom, which means we also need to celebrate the uniqueness of others. "I love that you are achieving success with that method. I am going to do things this way because it's a better fit for me."

That's wisdom. That's part of the calculation that helps us live out our authentic selves.

CHAPTER 9

BOOST YOUR
IMPACT

I gnition."

On the morning of April 7, 2001, the launch vehicle for the *Mars Odyssey* orbiter completed its prelaunch sequence and fired its engines. What happened next was an incredible feat of modern engineering. I'm not a rocket scientist myself, so I won't go into too many details here. But I think the main stages of that rocket launch are worth exploring.

What we typically call a *rocket* (the technical term is *launch vehicle*) was actually made up of of three separate stages stacked on top of each other. The first stage was 86 feet tall and 8 feet in diameter. So it was huge. And it was packed to the brim with more than 200,000 pounds of rocket fuel. The whole setup was basically a massive explosion contained in a tube and pointing upward.

But here's the crazy thing. All that fuel wasn't enough to get the launch vehicle where it needed to go. In addition to the main stage, there were nine boosters strapped to the sides of the primary rocket. Six of the boosters fired with the main stage at the time of ignition, and they kept firing for sixty-seven seconds before cutting out and dropping off. Then at two minutes and twelve seconds after launch, the final three boosters fired—a final burst of power that pushed the rocket out of our atmosphere and into outer space.

At that point, the first stage was finished. But there were still two stages to go.

The second stage rocket was 8 feet in diameter and 20 feet long. It was stuffed with a crazy mixture of fuel ingredients with crazy names—hydrazine and unsymmetrical dimethyl hydrazine and an oxidizer called nitrogen tetroxide. That rocket burned through its fuel in order to place the launch vehicle in a stable orbit around our planet.

The third and final stage was the smallest. It was just another booster, really—only 4 feet wide and 12 feet long. But when it ignited at just the right time, it sent the Mars orbiter careening out of earth's orbit and on a collision course with an entirely new planet.[1]

Think about that for a moment. The first rocket with its 200,000 pounds of fuel propelled the orbiter about 77 miles from Cape Canaveral, Florida, through the upper reaches of our atmosphere. The second rocket got the vehicle into orbit so it could be steered more easily. But it was that third rocket—the little booster—that made the biggest difference. That third rocket took the orbiter an incredible distance of 285 million miles until it finally reached Mars.

My point is that sometimes even a little boost can provide huge results when you're pointed in the right direction.

By this point in the book, I sincerely hope you're pointed in the right direction. You've worked hard to *understand* the concepts at play—that your *unique design*, *unique discontent*, *unique dreams*, and *unique destiny* are all part of what it means to live authentically in this world. You have *embraced* the value of your unique identity not just as a concept but as something that is true of you. And you are in the process of learning to *unleash* your unique identity through action so you can make your impact in the world.

My goal in this chapter is to provide a boost to help you break through. More accurately, I want to

> Sometimes even a little boost can provide huge results when you're pointed in the right direction.

offer three assets you can use to turbocharge your efforts as you unleash your unique identity. Those assets are confidence, context, and counsel.

One important clarification. For much of this book we have been discussing resources that are specific to each individual. Your mix of natural talents, gifts, and acquired skills is specific to you. It's part of your uniqueness. The same is true for the intangible qualities you bring to the table. Using the imagery from David and Goliath, nobody in the world carries the same bag of stones that you carry.

The assets we'll explore in this chapter, however, are available to all people. Everyone can learn to be *confident*. Everyone can use the power of *context*. And everyone can avail themselves of wise *counsel*. That definitely includes you, so let's get started.

CONFIDENCE

The first asset that can boost our ability to live authentically is *confidence*. But it's going to take some drilling down to get on the same page before we can truly explore the benefits of that asset. Why? Because a concept as vague as *confidence* can be difficult to pin down.

It's similar to the concept of *tallness*. All of us agree about what it means to be tall on a general level. We understand that a tall person is someone who is above average in height. When it comes to specifics, though, everybody has their own opinion. Should a six-foot man be considered tall? What about a six-foot woman? Among elementary teachers, a six-foot-four person might be extraordinarily tall. But among NBA players, six-four is average at best.

See what I mean? A concept like tallness is generally easy to process but difficult to pin down as soon as we try to be specific.

The same is true for confidence. There are many people who conflate confidence with cockiness or arrogance. Others view confidence as an intrepid quality that bolsters courage.

For the purpose of this book, I want to define confidence as "a belief in oneself." And yes, I recognize even that term is problematic because our culture has spent decades telling us to "believe in yourself" without giving any concrete reasons for that belief. It's one of those things we hear in Hallmark commercials and from commencement speakers. "Follow your heart." "Chase your dreams." "Believe in yourself."

Let me be clear. There's no value in believing in yourself the same way children believe in Santa Claus. Belief on its own brings nothing to the table, nor does verbalizing the phrase "I believe" cause anything to happen by itself.

Real belief is based on a foundation that is tangible. Just like faith.

So when I talk about confidence as a belief in self, I'm not describing something that is wishy-washy or disconnected from reality. Nor am I describing an attitude that is arrogant, where I view myself as the source of my own strength or as the only one who determines whether I am effective in unleashing my unique identity.

Rather, this confidence is the belief that your Creator did not make a mistake when he determined who you would be and what you would do. It's a belief that your Creator was effectual when he equipped you with your specific set of talents, gifts, skills, and intangible qualities. And it's a belief that you were equipped with those resources in order to carry out and complete specific assignments—and to complete them well. With excellence.

Belief in self is not hoping you can pull yourself up by your own bootstraps whenever you face difficult situations. Instead, it is understanding and accepting the truth that you've already been outfitted with the resources you will need to overcome those difficult situations; therefore, you can engage those battles with an expectation of victory.

That is the kind of belief that builds confidence. And that kind of confidence will be a rocket booster for your ability to unleash your unique identity.

When I think of my own life, I benefit greatly from this confidence—this belief in myself—in the realm of public speaking. I know a lot of people are freaked out by the thought of public speaking. It's a source of fear for a majority of the population. But it's a myth to think that public speakers are somehow exempt from that fear, doubt, or worry about embarrassing themselves.

I'm not exempt. I still experience a degree of trepidation when I step up to a platform to speak. Every time I go onstage, I am aware of what could happen if I mess up. Yet I am able to overcome those fears because I am confident that God created me to go up on that stage. He equipped me to be effective as a communicator. More than that, he called me to instruct and inspire the world, which means I would be turning my back on him *and on myself* if I gave in to those fears.

That knowledge creates confidence, and that confidence boosts my ability to be effective in unleashing myself and my resources wherever I am called to do so.

You can benefit from that same confidence when it comes to your purpose and calling because you also are equipped with everything you need to carry out that purpose and calling. You can believe in yourself because God created you with excellence.

Let's flesh that out a little bit. If you have a calling to teach, then you can engage the act of teaching with confidence. You've been equipped with knowledge and principles that are genuinely important. You are carrying information that your students really do need to know, and you are talented to relay that information in a way that is helpful—in a way that sticks. Sure, you may not see those "aha!" moments every day, but you can know with certainty that you are adding value to each student's life. You are helping them grow. You are making your difference in the world.

Or let's say you have a calling to serve. Your purpose is connected to laying aside your own needs and concerns so you can address the needs and concerns of others. If so, you can serve confidently. Not because you're so great, but because you've been greatly equipped. Greatly prepared. You don't need accolades or applause. You don't need recognition for your services, because you know those services are valuable. *You* are valuable; therefore, you will contribute to human flourishing in meaningful ways whenever you willingly give of yourself.

Whatever your calling happens to be, you can operate with confidence within that calling because you were created to do so. And the more you embrace this truth, the more your confidence will boost your effectiveness—which will, in turn, create more confidence.

We call that a virtuous cycle.

CONTEXT

Knowing and using the power of *context* is another rocket booster that can dramatically increase your ability to unleash your unique identity. By *context*, I mean the different circumstances and scenarios in which we operate as we seek to live out our purpose and calling.

Here's the issue. Some people equate being their authentic selves with behaving the same way in every context.

Sometimes this is unintentional. When someone is successfully doing something one way, it's easy to automatically keep doing that same thing the same way wherever they happen to be. For example, I read a story once about a corporate CEO who had retired. His wife was looking forward to spending a little more time together—which is why she was surprised when her husband announced an exploratory meeting the next Monday morning. Just for the two of them. The retired CEO confidently told his wife that he had a few ideas for increasing her efficiency around the house.

His wife responded by purchasing a she shed. For her eyes only.

Other times, though, people are intentionally inflexible. They don't want to be seen as inauthentic or wishy-washy, or they simply aren't willing to make the effort to change how they do things. Whatever the reason, every time they have an opportunity to unleash their resources, they do so in the same way.

That's a mistake.

For example, every time I speak in front of an audience, that audience hears from Dharius Daniels. If I speak at a seminary, I'm speaking as Dharius Daniels. When I preach on Sunday morning, I talk to my congregation as Dharius Daniels. When I'm on stage at a conference in the business space, I lead and train as Dharius Daniels.

I am the same person wherever I go—but what I say and what I do are not the same wherever I go. Why? Because each time an audience invites me to speak, I spend a lot of time answering this question: *What is the best way for me to unleash my gifts in this specific context? What is the best way for me to serve these specific people?*

Remember, you don't have a talent, gift, or skill, *singular*. You have a plethora of resources at your disposal. You have an arsenal filled with natural talents, spiritual gifts, acquired skills, and intangible qualities, *plural*—all of which are part of your unique identity. Therefore, part of unleashing your unique identity is determining which elements from that arsenal—which "stones" from your shepherd's bag—are going to be most effective in any given situation.

Once again, the story of David provides a great example. We know from Scripture that David was a skilled musician. That was part of his arsenal—part of his gifting. He even used that natural talent to soothe King Saul on several occasions:

> David came to Saul and entered his service. Saul liked him very much, and David became one of his armor-bearers. Then Saul sent word to Jesse, saying, "Allow David to remain in my service, for I am pleased with him."
> Whenever the spirit from God came on Saul, David would take up his lyre and play. Then relief would come

to Saul; he would feel better, and the evil spirit would leave him. (1 Samuel 16:21-23)

We spent a lot of time in the previous chapter exploring David's battle against Goliath. So just for a moment, imagine David had walked out to meet the giant carrying his lyre instead of his sling. On the one hand, it could have made sense. Music was part of David's unique identity, and he had already used that gift to win over someone who was bigger and stronger and more experienced than himself. You could make an argument for David trying the same tactic against the giant.

On the other hand, of course it would make no sense for David to face down an antagonistic giant using only a ukulele. Attempting to do so would be using the wrong resource for the situation at hand.

Here's the principle: *You and I can maximize our effectiveness when we understand the context in which we are operating. Understanding our context will allow us to choose and use the best resources.*

There's another element worth discussing—namely, *control*. By that, I mean having the discipline to unleash our gifts and our resources only when it will be helpful—and especially when those gifts and resources will produce a maximum impact.

Back to David. Notice that he didn't walk around chucking stones left and right with his sling. He didn't go out looking for reasons to crack people on the head. Nor did he constantly show off his skills with the lyre. "Want to hear a song?"

No, David was disciplined. He budgeted himself and his resources in a way that demonstrated control.

Am I saying we should be stingy with our gifts and resources? Am I saying we should keep to ourselves so people won't bother us or expect anything from us? No.

Remember, I want you to *unleash* your unique identity. I want you to get out there and make your difference in the world. I want you to authentically live out who you are so you can accomplish what you were created to accomplish, and that means being generous with the talents, gifts, and skills that are part of your unique design.

But sometimes we confuse being generous with being indiscriminate. Sometimes we conflate making *our* difference, which is specific and targeted, with trying to stick our nose and our resources into *everyone else's* business. That's a bad idea. That's poor stewardship. That's not helpful to others, and it's not helpful to ourselves.

All of this points back to purpose and calling. You were created in a specific way so you can solve specific problems. By understanding the importance of context and by demonstrating discipline in the way you unleash your resources—by unleashing in a way that is under control—you will be much more effective in addressing the problems you were created to solve and thereby make your difference in the world.

COUNSEL

David ruled as Israel's king after the death of Saul and his sons. David wasn't perfect, but he was effective for the majority of his reign. The people loved him, and the nation flourished for decades in terms of wealth, prestige, stability, and even geographical expansion. David was an excellent king.

Then things started to go off the rails. The story of David and Bathsheba is, arguably, David's greatest moral failure. After that event, David experienced a great deal of tumult and turmoil in his household. This chaos culminated with David's son Absalom temporarily seizing the throne from his father in a well-planned coup. Through various means, Absalom won the hearts of the people in Jerusalem. And in a deft maneuver, he gathered an army to attack the city so swiftly that David and his followers were forced to flee.

Having said all that, look at this interaction between David and Hushai, one of the king's advisers:

> When David arrived at the summit, where people used to worship God, Hushai the Arkite was there to meet him, his robe torn and dust on his head. David said to him, "If you go with me, you will be a burden to me. But if you return to the city and say to Absalom, 'Your Majesty, I will be your servant; I was your father's servant in the past, but now I will be your servant,' then you can help me by frustrating Ahithophel's advice. Won't the priests Zadok and Abiathar be there with you? Tell them anything you hear in the king's palace. Their two sons, Ahimaaz son of Zadok and Jonathan son of Abiathar, are there with them. Send them to me with anything you hear."
>
> So Hushai, David's confidant, arrived at Jerusalem as Absalom was entering the city. (2 Samuel 15:32–37)

Obviously, that was some CIA-level spy craft from David, even in a stressful moment. David didn't want his rival to receive good advice from Ahithophel, who was a noted strategist. So David sent his own counselor undercover in order to give Absalom bad advice and frustrate the whole situation.

These verses in Scripture prove that David understood the value of *wise counsel*. You and I need to have the same understanding if we want to unleash our unique identity.

This principle is important to me, but not just because

coaching is a key part of my ministry. It's important within the pages of this book. Why? Because I don't want you to hear me talking about *your* unique identity, *your* resources, and *your* strengths and think that *you* are the answer to all of your problems. I don't want to give you the impression that you have everything it takes to unleash your authentic self all wrapped up in your own brain.

You don't. You (and I too) need help. Specifically, your ability to make your impact in the world will receive a turbo-boost when you avail yourself of wise counsel. Remember the words of Solomon, another son of David: "For lack of guidance a nation falls, but victory is won through many advisers" (Proverbs 11:14).

One more qualification. When I talk about *receiving* coaching and counsel, I don't want to give the impression that this is a purely passive experience. I'm not suggesting you determine what your options are in a given situation, present those options to coaches you trust, and then say, "Tell me what to do." That's not an effective way to boost your resources.

Instead, I'm talking about counsel as an active and ongoing conversation. Yes, part of that conversation means listening to people who have more experience than you do and are a little wiser than you are. But it's also necessary to be around peers who know you and know your situation, and with whom you can engage in some back-and-forth discussion.

Remember in chapter 7 when I talked about forging your tribe? About actively finding people who have a purpose and calling similar to your own? That's another part of benefiting from counsel and coaching. Be around people who understand your wheelhouse so that you can boost one another and push each other forward with exponential results.

HOW TO BUILD YOUR BOOSTERS

"How can I develop these important assets?"

If there's one question I hear more than others after a speaking engagement or conference or worship service, it's that one. *How?* "How do I do what you just said?" When people resonate with a principle or a concept they believe will be helpful in their lives, they naturally want to get specific instructions on how to implement that principle or concept.

I applaud that impulse. That desire. Changing the direction of your life requires more than information; it takes action.

Yet it can be difficult to show someone exactly how to do something without a deeper understanding of that person's situation—their resources, experiences, obstacles, and so on. That's why I believe in coaching as much as I do. Coaching and other forms of mentorship allow for specific instructions that are tailored to individual needs.

Still, I do want to address the "how?" question whenever possible. We've done that throughout these pages, and I want to do it here by suggesting some general, practical steps you can take to gain confidence, use the power of context, and find wise counsel.

How to Gain Confidence

Many people mistakenly try to boost their own confidence through an act of willpower. The most common form of this phenomenon is an individual standing in front of the mirror and crying out, "You can do this! You can do this!"

In my experience, these kinds of self-motivational techniques won't take you very far. Instead, gaining confidence typically boils down to two important words: *failure* and *success*.

For starters, you need to understand that nothing kills your confidence faster than failure. Nothing. Failure can drain away our confidence, and even our desire to try again, into what seems like a black hole. Why? Because failure is painful. It hurts to mess up, and when we do, it makes us hesitate whenever we muster up the nerve to try again—because we don't want to experience that pain again.

That tendency is magnified a hundredfold whenever we fail in front of other people. The only thing worse than failing is failing publicly.

So although it may sound strange, one of the best ways to boost your confidence is to learn how to effectively manage failure—in fact, learning how to use failure as a resource and even as a benefit.

The trick is to embrace the reality that every failure is an opportunity to learn a lesson. You may have heard what Thomas Edison was reported to have said after inventing the light bulb after one thousand failed attempts: "I didn't fail one thousand times; I've just found one thousand ways that won't work." Or something like that. Yes, it's corny. Yes, it's a bit of an oversimplification. Yes, it's an overused illustration.

But it's also true. And helpful for managing failure. That's because every time you fail at something important—every time you fail at a task or an effort connected with your calling—you are given another opportunity to learn how to do it better next time. Each failure is a lesson that shows you how to improve on your next attempt.

Managing our failures will boost our confidence when we embrace the truth that failure is part of the process for success. Failure is a *necessary* step on the journey toward achievement. It really is that simple.

Remember, your confidence is not based on your ability to

do well. Instead, it's based on the reality that you were created specifically to excel at your calling and achieve your purpose. Your confidence rests not in you but in the One who designed you. Your Creator designed you to succeed.

So the next time you fail at something important, stop. Take a step back and assess what specifically went wrong? Why did it go wrong? And most importantly, what can you learn from that experience? What adjustment can you make to avoid that specific failure in the future? Taking the time to learn those lessons and adjust your approach will turn failure into a confidence booster.

> Each failure is a lesson that shows you how to improve.

You can also build confidence by following a similar process when you succeed. Sometimes we feel relieved when things go well. *Whew! That was great because I didn't fail.* Again, this is the wrong approach.

Your calling and your purpose are proof that you were designed to succeed when you apply your talents, gifts, and skills to the problems you were created to solve. Therefore, success should be your expectation. It's a given. It's going to happen.

When you succeed, take a step back. Evaluate the experience. What specifically went well in that moment? What did you do that led to success? What obstacles got in your way, and how were they overcome? What lessons can you learn from the experience that will pave the way to even bigger victories in the future?

Learning to manage failure and success will keep you focused on the reality that you belong. That you are designed with purpose. And remaining focused on that reality will boost your confidence.

How to Navigate Context

We want to avoid using the same methods and the same resources in every context. Remember, being your authentic self does not mean doing the same thing in every situation. Instead, you can maximize each opportunity to unleash your unique identity by selecting the best resources for that specific moment—in that specific context.

So on a practical level, the first step you need to take to maximize your resources is determining the resources that are available to you. In other words, you must figure out what stones are in your bag.

A number of tools can help you identify your resources. I like the *CliftonStrengths* talent assessment and the *Now, Discover Your Strengths* book from Gallup, but there are many others.[2]

Thinking specifically about your purpose and your unique identity, we've been dividing your resources into four categories throughout these pages:

- natural talents and abilities
- spiritual gifts
- acquired skills
- intangible qualities

To help you maximize the power of context, I strongly recommend you take an inventory of the weapons in your arsenal. Grab four pieces of paper and label each one according to the categories above. Then write out what you've got. Write down your natural talents. Write down your spiritual gifts. Write down the skills you have acquired over the years through opposition and opportunity. And write down those "weird" intangible qualities that make you who you are.

What you are doing in this exercise is assessing yourself. You are taking inventory of the resources at your disposal.

The next step to using the power of context is to assess your opportunities to use these resources. Think of this as "reading the room." Think critically and pragmatically about the circumstances in which you will be unleashing your unique identity—and do that thinking *before* you find yourself attempting to do the unleashing.

Let's say you have a calling to write. You are a content creator of some sort. Navigating context means identifying the people you are attempting to inform or influence before you begin that process of creation. Much of this is demographics. Who will be reading what you produce? What are their ages? What is their level of education?

But your main goal in this process is to identify the needs of the people you are trying to serve. What problems are they trying to solve? What are they looking for and hoping for when they seek out what you've written? In what ways do they want you to help?

These types of questions aren't limited to writing or speaking or other roles that involve an audience in a more traditional sense. These questions apply to every opportunity you have to unleash your unique identity.

If you have a calling to lead, for example, you need to assess the people who are following you. That's your context, and there can be wildly different contexts connected to different groups of people—employees, volunteers, students, seniors, people looking for some fun, people in crisis, and so on. If you have a calling as a financial adviser to make sure people are equipped for the present and the future, you will have different opportunities to make a difference, depending on the different needs and preparedness of different clients. If you have audiences on YouTube or other forms of social media, you will need to adapt your strategies for using your resources in a way that best fits each of these specific audiences. And so on and so forth.

How to Find Wise Counsel

"How do I find the right coach? How do I get someone to mentor me?" This is probably the category of question I hear most often from people.

In my experience, there are three basic ways to avail yourself of wise counsel in a serious way: show up, support, and sow. Let's tackle those one at a time.

The first way to find wise counsel is to *show up*. As I mentioned earlier, I lived for many years as if I expected wise mentors or potential members of my tribe to knock on my door and ask to be invited into my life. Obviously, that didn't happen. It wasn't until I began to actively look for my tribe and wise mentors that I started to find them.

The same is true for you. Don't sit still and wait for helpful people to come into your life. Instead, get up and go out to where those helpful people are already operating. In other words, show up.

To do this, you first need to clarify what kind of people you are looking for. Ask yourself these basic questions:

- Who are the types of people that would be especially helpful to be around? (Older people with experience in my field? Peers who understand the challenges I'm facing?)
- Where can I find these people? (What events attract them? What associations or groups are they a part of? Where do they spend their time?)

- What can I do to go where these people are? (What upcoming events in my community would attract these people? What groups could I join?)

Again, the key words here are *intention* and *action*. You have the ability to connect with people who can be helpful in your life. You just need to be intentional about finding these people and active in showing up where they are.

The second way to avail yourself of wise counsel is to *support*. This is especially important when you're looking for a coach or a mentor.

I'm going to say something here that may sound harsh, but I believe it's helpful. In my experience, many people approach potential mentors in the wrong way because they do so with their hands out asking for help. The coach or mentor has something of value, and the person seeking counsel does so in a posture of receiving. *Give me what I need.*

I have encountered many people with that posture who wanted my help. "Dharius, here are the problems I'm facing in my career. Will you help me?" "Dharius, I don't know what I'm supposed to be doing with my life. Will you mentor me?" "Dharius, I'm facing this particular crisis. Can you tell me what to do?"

I usually find such requests off-putting. It's not because I don't want to help others. I do. It's not because I don't care about people. I care very much. And it's not because I don't think I could be of assistance. Chances are quite good that I could help.

The reason I typically resist those who seek me out with a "please, help me!" approach is that I have found they often become a drain on my resources. Remember, I have my own calling. I have my own responsibility to unleash my unique identity in a way that makes my difference in the world. Therefore I've learned I must be selective and disciplined by focusing my efforts on those opportunities that will create the biggest difference—which typically doesn't include solving individual problems.

Now flip the script. There have been times when people approach me, not with a self-serving attitude, but with a desire to support. "Dharius, I see what you are doing in the world is valuable. How can I help? How can I support you?"

Whoa. That's different. Those are the types of people I am excited to give my time and attention to. Does that make me selfish? No. It makes me a good steward of the resources I've been given. I want to invest in opportunities that produce results both for myself and those who are seeking a mentor or a coach.

Having said all that, here is my practical advice if you are seeking a coach or mentor to help you get to the next level. Don't approach a potential coach or mentor seeking a handout. Instead, approach them by offering a hand up. Give of yourself to support what that person is doing, and you will receive an exponential reward in what comes back your way. I promise.

Finally, the third way to avail yourself of wise counsel is to *sow*—meaning, pay to play. Invest financial or other resources to secure what you need.

Many coaches and mentors offer their services for a fee. This doesn't make them selfish or unspiritual. It simply means they have something of value to offer, and they understand they should rightly be compensated for offering it. In a similar way, several memberships or associations require a financial investment in order to join. Paying to avail yourself of these resources can be a wonderful investment when they allow greater access to community and counsel.

Remember, all of these boosts are predicated on you being pointed in the right direction. When you have a strong sense of your calling and purpose—of who you were created to be and what you were created to do—you can maximize your impact in your community and the world by gaining confidence, navigating the power of context, and seeking out wise counsel.

CHAPTER 10

GO GET IT

Would you like to step into my office?

I've mentioned a few times already that coaching is an important part of my life. I've benefited many times from the wisdom and counsel of quality coaches. And I've made it a priority for many years now to serve others as a coach. It's a big part of what I do.

As I've been pondering how to frame the final chapter of this book, I wondered what I might say and what I might do if you and I were connected through a coaching relationship. We've been working together for nine chapters now. We've covered topics that I know are intensely personal and that I hope will be profoundly productive, both for you and for me. So how would I like to wrap things up if we were in that context? How would I send you forth in the hopes that you will become the person you were created to be and accomplish all that you were created to do?

Let's find out. Walk with me through the door and sit down in this comfortable chair while I hop behind my desk.

If it helps you to visualize the space, my office is fairly spartan—not a lot of decorations on the walls or knickknacks covering my shelves. The thing that dominates my office from a visual perspective is a huge map of the world, which has been painted on my back wall in black-and-white—a daily reminder that I have been called to impact the world for the kingdom of Jesus Christ.

As we get started on this final coaching session, you should know I'm not a big rah-rah guy. I'm not going to jump up and down or yell or use a bunch of gimmicks to try to keep your attention. That's not me.

But I am going to give you my full attention. I am going to lean forward and look into your eyes as we speak. I'm going to share what's on my heart and in my mind with passion and with enthusiasm, because these concepts matter to me. You matter to me.

Are you ready to get started? There are three takeaways that I believe are crucial for you to consider as we wrap up this exploration of *unique identity*—three steps I want us to contemplate together before you walk out that door: (1) I want you to define who you are; (2) I want you to determine your "why"; and (3) I want you to decide what to do next. Let's go get it.

DEFINE WHO YOU ARE

You and I are in a bit of an awkward place for this conversation because we do not know each other. I assume you may have heard a little about me, simply given that you are reading this book. But I don't know you. I don't know your history. I don't know what you look like. I don't even know your name.

Yet there are many things I do know about you. Important things. Foundational truths that I know for certain about the core of who you are, and I know them even if you are unaware of those truths yourself.

For example, I know you have a *unique identity*. You are different from the world around you, and you have felt that difference your entire life. You are unique. There's a chance your uniqueness has seemed like a bad thing for much of your life, but it's actually a great thing. It is a wonderful gift.

I also know you have a *unique design*. You are not a random amalgamation of cells and sinews and organ systems. Instead, you are the product of celestial blueprints that were determined before the first atom existed in our universe, and you were knit together with divine precision and divine creativity according to a divine timeline. You are the culmination of a plan. And according to that plan, you now carry within you a powerful arsenal of natural talents, spiritual gifts, acquired skills, and intangible qualities that are uniquely yours. Nobody else was designed like you or equipped like you.

I know you've had (and will continue to have) moments in your life when you've experienced a *unique discontent*. You feel uniquely bothered by certain problems—irritated by issues that seem to affect you considerably more than they affect other people. And that is true because those are the problems and issues you were created to solve.

I know you've had (and will continue to have) moments in your life when you've become aware of your *unique dreams*. These are moments when you wake up. When you feel really and truly alive. I advise you to pay attention to those moments, because the opportunities that inspire you are often those you were created to seize. These dreams and desires are part of what makes you who you are, and pursuing these dreams is crucial if you are to experience a life of meaning and fulfillment.

I know you have a *unique destiny*. I don't know what your

destiny is specifically, and you may not either. That's okay. Your Creator knows because he designed you for that destiny. He designed you to make an ultimate contribution to human flourishing—a contribution that only you can provide. I know you have the choice right now to either walk toward that destiny or push it farther away.

Let's keep it rolling because I also know you are a person of *tremendous value*. How do I know that? Because you are a child of God. Maybe that sounds corny, but it's true. You have been created in God's image and you bear his name—his seal of approval.

In the town of Lowestoft, England, a building was listed for sale at roughly $400,000. There were no buyers, largely because the building was a bit run-down. It even had a bunch of graffiti painted on one wall. Then, strangely, the building's owner changed the sale price—to almost $700,000. Why the massive increase? Because one of the graffiti pictures (a mural of a child carrying a crowbar) had been confirmed as the work of Banksy, a prominent yet secretive painter. In other words, the building's value almost doubled simply because it had been marked by a famous artist.[1]

Well, you have been marked by the Creator of the universe. You are his work of art. Therefore I know you carry tremendous value.

Finally, I know you have a *purpose*. You were created not simply to "be" but to accomplish. You are here for a reason. You have been gifted and equipped for a reason.

Those are all things I know to be true about you, and I hope by now that you are convinced of these truths as well. Each of these elements is part of what makes you unique—part of what makes you special. But only you can articulate the full picture. Only you can clearly define who you are and what you were created to achieve.

That's what I want you to do right now—define yourself. Use the space below to write down who you were created to be and what you were created to do.

_____

_____

_____

_____

I use the word *define* here intentionally, because it carries a sense of permanence. A lot of new words are added to the dictionary every year. Recently words like *dad bod* and *amirite* have made it in, which is a bit depressing, I know. Still, once a word officially makes it into the dictionary, it's typically locked in. That definition rarely changes.

So once you have defined who you are, lock in that definition. Make it permanent. Don't let anyone or anything pressure you to change what you know to be true about you.

DETERMINE YOUR "WHY"

There's a phrase I often encounter in my work as a life coach that I believe is important for you to hear. It goes like this: "'Why power' is more important than willpower."

The "why" in that phrase is connected to the reasons you do what you do. Specifically, it refers to the reasons you are endeavoring to make a big change or accomplish something significant. It's your motivation for action. So the principle is that your motivation for reaching toward important goals or changes will be more important—more useful and empowering—than simply gritting your teeth and trying to "will" yourself into proper behavior through strength of mind.

"Why power" is more important than willpower.

In the context of this book, your "why" includes all the incentives for you to understand, embrace, and unleash your unique identity. I'm talking about the motives behind your effort to be who you were created to be and do what you were created to do.

Why is "why power" necessary? Because anytime you try to make a big change or accomplish something significant, a moment will come when you hit a wall. Probably several moments and several walls. Which means there will be obstacles. There will be unexpected opposition. It doesn't matter if you're trying to learn a new language, lose weight, gain weight, rebuild finances, fix a marriage, earn a promotion—whatever it is, obstacles will come.

Anytime you reach for something big, you are going to hit a wall. And it's your "why" that will get you through the wall.

So I want you to put your "why" into words. I want you to express the reasons and the motivations for unleashing your unique identity. And I'm going to help you do that by asking you to answer two questions: (1) What will happen and (2) what won't happen?

Identify What Will Happen

First, I want you to identify what will happen as you continue this process of understanding, embracing, and unleashing your unique identity. What benefits will you reap as you become who you were created to be and do what you were created to do?

How will moving in that direction affect you as a person? How will it influence your spiritual life? What emotions will you experience as things start to click and you find yourself making the impact you've always wanted to make?

What will happen in your family when you unleash your unique identity? How will this unleashing affect your closest relationships? What opportunities will your authentic lifestyle open up for the people you love most? What opportunities will you have to serve and support these people?

Now think about your community—maybe it's your neighborhood, maybe your church, maybe your workplace and social spaces all wrapped up together. Whatever it is, how will you be able to influence your community as you unleash your unique identity? Where will you have the chance to make a difference? Whom can you bless? What problems will you be able to solve or address in a meaningful way?

You get my point by now. Part of your "why" is identifying the positive changes that you and others will experience as you grow in your ability to live authentically and make *your* impact in the world.

That's huge.

Identify What Won't Happen

But the positive stuff is only half of your "why." I also want you to think about what won't happen if you step back and shrug off all the principles we have addressed in these pages. What won't happen if you choose not to unleash your unique identity?

Again, let's start with you. What are some dreams or goals that would be in danger of slipping away if you choose to conform to who others expect you to be and if you choose to do what others expect you to do? How will your life be affected if you fail to make your ultimate contribution to human flourishing? What emotions will you carry if you never identify or achieve your purpose?

What about your family? Think of the people who love you

most and want the best for you. How will they be impacted if you turn away from pursuing that best? How will they be changed if your life is mediocre when both you and they know that it could be marvelous? How will future generations remember you if you decide not to pursue your destiny?

Think once again about your community. What are some problems you were created to solve, and what will happen if you choose not to solve them? What are some contributions you were created to make in this world, and what will happen to you and to the world if you choose to withhold those contributions?

These aren't fun thoughts. I know that. But they are important because they can keep you pointed in the right direction when circumstances threaten to knock you off track.

All of this is your "why." So keep hold of it. Write it down. Remember it. Remind yourself of it regularly—weekly or even daily if possible.

Because it's your "why" that is going to get you through the walls.

DECIDE WHAT TO DO

One of the main reasons I enjoy reading books (and writing books, for that matter) is that they provide helpful information. They give us access to knowledge we did not possess previously and allow us the opportunity to engage and wrestle with critical concepts.

More than just information, though, the best books give us options. They provide pathways not just for thinking differently but for living differently. That has certainly been my goal in these pages.

Right now, you have three options for how to respond after you close these pages for the final time:

1. You can do nothing.
2. You can take the information we've explored, think about it, and tell yourself you're going to do something about it later.
3. You can take quick and massive action so you can achieve massive results.

I'm hoping you'll choose the third option. I encourage you not to delay when it comes to grabbing hold of who you were created to be, so you can accomplish all you were designed to achieve.

Because there is much at stake.

Recently I read the story of a man named George Dawson, who was born in 1898. His grandfather had been a slave. Dawson himself began his working career at the age of four. No school for him or his siblings. His life was a long line of ups and downs, underscored by hard work, the love of family, and decades of monotony.

Then came a change. When Dawson was ninety-eight years old, a literacy volunteer knocked on the door of his home in South Dallas. When the young person told the old man that adult education courses were being taught just a few blocks away, Dawson was enthusiastic. "Wait," he said, "I'll get my coat."

Dawson started by learning to read and write. He wanted to sign his name with more than an *X*, and he learned to do so with a flourish. He kept studying and earned his GED. Then he wrote a book! He was more than a hundred years old when it was published, and it gave him the chance to share his story through venues such as *The Oprah Winfrey Show* and *Good Morning America*. He was profiled in *People* magazine.[2]

The title of the book is *Life Is So Good*.[3]

Today you can visit George Dawson Middle School in Southlake, Texas, just outside Dallas. The name was changed as an acknowledgment of and tribute to the legacy of a man who understood there's never a wrong time to become who you were created to be.

When I first heard George Dawson's story, I felt both encouraged and challenged. I was encouraged because it confirmed the truth that it's never too late to unleash your stone. It's never too late to live authentically. Even if you were to wait until you were ninety-eight years old, you could still make your impact in the world.

Dawson's story is a challenge because it forces us to grapple with a crucial question: *What could happen if I don't wait?*

What could happen if you decide you will not wait decades to try to achieve something meaningful? What could happen if you don't wait until you're more experienced? Better educated? More financially secure? What could you accomplish if you don't wait until the kids are out of the house? Or until you hit retirement and free up some spare time?

I'm talking about unleashing who you are. I'm talking about choosing to live as the person you've always known you were created to be. I'm talking about striving—not walking casually but running with all your strength—toward the purpose you know deep down you were created to achieve.

What would happen if you chose to make quick and massive changes in your life today? Right now. Right this moment. What could you accomplish with the rest of your life?

I'm praying we both find out.

ACKNOWLEDGMENTS

I often say we don't go as far as our dream; we go as far as our team. This has been the case for this book.

My gratitude goes out to the following:

- First of all, to my incredible wife, who is one of God's greatest gifts to me.
- To a hidden hero, Dr. Joseph Umidi, who taught me the framework I used in this book. He showed me the importance of recognizing our unique designs, unique dreams, and unique destiny.
- To my incredible agent, Shannon Marven, from Dupree Miller for all of her wisdom, guidance, and advocacy.
- To the amazing team at Zondervan for their incredible partnership.
- To my friend and partner, Marc Jeffrey, who has worked with me on every book I've published. I really believe the best is yet to come.

NOTES

Introduction
1. See Psalm 139:13–16; Ephesians 2:10.

Chapter 1: Your Unique Design
1. Emily Brignone et al., "Trends in the Diagnosis of Diseases of Despair in the United States, 2009–2018: A Retrospective Cohort Study," *BMJ Open* 10, no. 10, https://bmjopen.bmj.com /content/10/10/e037679.info.
2. "Facts and Statistics," Anxiety and Depression Association of America, https://adaa.org/understanding-anxiety/facts -statistics.
3. "Laboratory-Confirmed COVID-19-Associated Hospitalizations," Centers for Disease Control and Prevention, https://gis.cdc .gov/grasp/COVIDNet/COVID19_3.html.
4. "Opioid Crisis Statistics," Health and Human Services, www .hhs.gov/opioids/about-the-epidemic/opioid-crisis-statistics /index.html.
5. Cited in "How Often Do You Feel Lonely?" Statista (February 2021), www.statista.com/statistics/1222815/loneliness-among -adults-by-country.

6. "Loneliness and Social Isolation Linked to Serious Health Conditions," Centers for Disease Control and Prevention, www .cdc.gov/aging/publications/features/lonely-older-adults.html.

Chapter 2: Unique Discontent

1. Quoted in "William Wilberforce: Antislavery Politician," *Christian History* 53 (1997), www.christianitytoday.com/history /people/activists/william-wilberforce.html.
2. Quoted in "William Wilberforce," *Christian History*.
3. To read the full story of the fall of Jerusalem, check out 2 Kings 24:1–25:26.

Chapter 3: Unique Dreams

1. See Jacqueline Howard, "Myron Rolle's Journey from NFL to Neurosurgery," CNN, May 22, 2017, www.cnn.com/2017/05/19 /health/myron-rolle-nfl-medical-school-profile/index.html.
2. "Welcome to Real Rap with Reynolds!" YouTube, January 27, 2019, www.youtube.com/watch?v=vkcMeaVVbrE.

Chapter 4: Your Unique Destiny

1. Quoted in Doug Criss, "He Donated Blood Every Week for 60 Years and Saved the Lives of 2.4 Million Babies," CNN, December 25, 2018, www.cnn.com/2018/05/11/health/james -harrison-blood-donor-retires-trnd/index.html.
2. Quoted in NPR Staff, "'Man with the Golden Arm' Donates Blood That Has Saved 2 Million Babies," NPR: All Things Considered, June 14, 2015, www.npr.org/2015/06/14/414397424 /man-with-the-golden-arm-donates-blood-thats-saved-2-million -babies.
3. Quoted in Criss, "He Donated Blood."
4. See Robert Frank, "Elon Musk Is Now the Richest Person in the World, Passing Jeff Bezos," CNBC, January 7, 2021, www .cnbc.com/2021/01/07/elon-musk-is-now-the-richest-person -in-the-world-passing-jeff-bezos-.html.

5. See Paul Rincon, "What Is Elon Musk's Starship?" BBC News, November 17, 2021, https://www.bbc.com/news/science-environment-55564448.

6. Simon Sinek, "The Millennial Question," YouTube, December 30, 2016, www.youtube.com/watch?v=vudaAYx2IcE.

7. Lebron James, who currently plays basketball for the Los Angeles Lakers, is now thirty-seven years old. He entered the National Basketball Association as a rookie at the age of eighteen in 2003.

Chapter 5: Embrace Who You Are

1. See Crystal Raypole, "Yes, You Can (and Should) Give Yourself a Hug," Healthline, June 16, 2020, www.healthline.com/health/hugging-self.

Chapter 6: Evaluate How You Got Here

1. To read the full story of Moses's early life, check out Exodus 2:1–25.

Chapter 8: Take Your Shot

1. Guy Raz, "What's the Real Story of David and Goliath?" NPR: TED Radio Hour, November 15, 2013, www.npr.org/transcripts/243294593.

2. Read 1 Samuel 17:34–37 for more about David's experiences in fighting things that were bigger and stronger than he was.

Chapter 9: Boost Your Impact

1. See "Launch Sequence Description," NASA: Mars Odyssey, https://mars.nasa.gov/odyssey/mission/timeline/mtlaunch/launch2.

2. For more information on these resources, visit www.gallup.com/cliftonstrengths/en/286556/ndys.aspx.

Chapter 10: Go Get It

1. Cited in Hannah Frishberg, "Banksy Art Ripped out of Building Wall by UK Landlord," *New York Post*, November 16,

2021, https://nypost.com/2021/11/16/banksy-art-ripped-out
-of-building-wall-by-uk-landlord.

2. See Myrna Oliver, "George Dawson: Author Learned to Read at
98," *Los Angeles Times*, July 7, 2001, www.latimes.com/archives
/la-xpm-2001-jul-07-me-19480-story.html.

3. George Dawson and Richard Glaubman, *Life Is So Good: One
Man's Extraordinary Journey through the Twentieth Century and How
He Learned to Read at Age 98* (New York: Random House, 2013).

Relational Intelligence

The People Skills You Need for the Life of Purpose You Want

Dr. Dharius Daniels

Relational Intelligence is your action plan for getting smart about who you surround yourself with. Using Jesus' relational framework for choosing the twelve disciples, this book gives you the tools you need to define, discern, align, assess, and activate your relationships to unlock your greatest potential.

Years of ministry leadership experience have taught Dr. Dharius Daniels that there's no such thing as a casual relationship. All of our relationships either push us forward into our God-given purposes or hold us back from who we're meant to be. If you're serious about taking your life to the next level, you should be serious about taking your relationships to the next level too.

Scripture gives us a blueprint for the way relationships should be managed, and this blueprint helps us construct and grow relationships that are fruitful. It tells us that our spiritual, physical, financial, emotional, and professional progress is greatly impacted by who we allow to be a part of our lives and what part we allow them to play. *Relational Intelligence* reminds us that with our destiny on the line, relationships are too consequential to nonchalantly roll the dice in managing them.

Dr. Daniels shows us that relationships were part of God's design, and when we understand and apply what God has to say about them, we can finally learn to:

- reflect on the people that God has placed in our lives;
- avoid unnecessary relational turmoil;
- be intentional in each of our relationships; and
- accomplish our God-given purpose.

When your purpose is on the line, the cost of relational unintelligence is too great to pay. Join Dr. Daniels as you uncover the secret to gaining the relational intelligence you need to build the purposeful life that you want.

Available in stores and online!